THE AGE OF INFORMATION

An Interdisciplinary Survey of Cybernetics

THE AGE OF INFORMATION

An Interdisciplinary Survey of Cybernetics

T. C. HELVEY

●

EDUCATIONAL TECHNOLOGY PUBLICATIONS

Englewood Cliffs, New Jersey 07632

Printed in the United States of America.

Library of Congress Catalog Card Number: 78-125870.

International Standard Book Number: 0-87778-008-0.

First Printing

Dedicated

to love and human compassion in general and to
Nora in particular.

Acknowledgement

It is a pleasure to express my gratitude to my friends, Drs. John Proctor, Ludwig von Bertalanffy and Heinz von Foerster, whose encouragement was one of the significant forcing functions in the control of the creation of this book.

PREFACE

The purpose of this book is to provide in one volume general information on Cybernetics and the related "interaction sciences."

It is quite a dilemma for an author to correlate the style, the topic, the level of presentation, the use and the number of technical terms and the scope of the manuscript for the reading public. One could write, for instance, a treatise for cyberneticians, wherein one could assume that the lingo of the profession will be understood and that the specific technical knowledge will be mastered by every reader. Regarding the relatively small number in that guild, this would restrict the circulation to an undesirable minimum. The other extreme is the popularized version for the layman. This type is often very rewarding, both educationally and economically.

This book, however, is written in the attempt to interest, on one hand, the scholar, but, on the other hand, to make the material accessible to the well-educated populace, whose prime interest is in other areas, but who wish to obtain information about cybernetics.

A glossary is added at the end of the book, and the corresponding words in the text are marked with an asterisk. This way, it is hoped, the book will be suitable for virtually all levels of technical comprehension.

Although it is felt by the writer that the means of communication must be advanced beyond the obsolete invention of Gutenberg—the folded book—no better tool is available, so far, from the shelves of bioengineers.

T.C. Helvey
Professor of Cybernetics
University of Tennessee Space Institute
Tullahoma, Tennessee

December, 1970

CONTENTS

THE AGE OF INFORMATION

An Interdisciplinary Survey of Cybernetics

1.

PROMETHEUS REINCARNATED

Some Fundamentals of Cybernetic Pedagogy and the New Systems Sciences in the Service of Democracy.

Until recently, the term "humanity" stood high as the Rock of Gibraltar over any form of organismic or technological entity. Many of the "unique" human characteristics, however, crumbled under the impassionate research results in animal behavior. Man had to admit that the beast possesses a goodly number of mental capabilities which are uncomfortably similar to those of his own. But, at least, the machine remained under his thumb. That was what he thought, with some arrogance, until the dawn of the intelligent machines.

Within a century (or maybe sooner), however, man's struggle for life will be shared to an ever-increasing degree by machine partners.

Beside the sophisticated technology of intelligent machines— their production and maintenance—the two great pylons around which will center man's interest are communication and education.

The reality of man's exo-environment* will depend on the fidelity and reliability of the telecommunication of sensible nature-elements; namely, the bits of information which he receives through his senses by a nature-machine-man triadic* system. The

3

trend of perfecting communication systems may yield strange aberrations. For instance, already some of the superb high fidelity recordings of Casals or Rubinstein have a better tone quality than when these masters are listened to in the concert hall.

Man will rely more and more on transmitted and decoded information, and his survival will not depend on his physical fitness, but on the quality of his communication system.

Furthermore, because he will be removed from the constant need of transfer functions* in a direct coupled control system, he will have to know how to utilize the machine partner's capabilities to satisfy his needs. This will require an immense volume of knowledge, which he must obtain by the process of education. The technique by which education can be acquired is called pedagogy. Thus, the same way as, for instance, for most people, vocational training or academic education is the *sine qua non** tool for today's happiness, in the future, cybernetic pedagogy will provide the means for human beings to live the life which is most beneficial for their times.

THE TREND

Certain devices are already on drawing boards that will read, or rather decipher, human-generated longhand scripts and then go about doing something intelligent with this information, provided the information content of the message is meaningful, in the sense that its content satisfies a truth test and is above *a priori* thresholds of credibility and amount. Consequent to the voice-control principle,* which has been available for some time, techniques are under development for picking up the audio waves generated when a man speaks, and changing these signals into a form that can be stored electromagnetically and reproduced in the form of a printed text. Research is progressing also on new, unusual ways of reaching the human senses by generating symbols for the eye to see or coded tones for the ear to hear, even certain vibrations to feel—so that information available in machines can be conveyed efficiently to the human intellect, regardless of how it was obtained or processed. On the other hand, thinking produces electrical impulses which can be amplified and coded; this can be a useful feedback signal to determine progress in cerebration.

To top these advances in Bionics,* we can willfully modify the output pattern of our brains, and, with the aid of a miniature pulse-height analyzer* and amplifier-transmitter, we can, by thinking, start or stop electronic equipment. Furthermore, by coding our brainwaves with an off-on key, we can directly transmit thoughts and intelligence from our brain to a Morse Code printer or teletyper. There is little doubt that later, by further sophistication of such technique, a brain-to-brain communication will be feasible; and, even if a miniature electronic transmitter and a sensor are necessary as a conveyer of signals, radically novel communication problems will become manifest.

All of this indicates our transition to a new, highly technological society, in which, however, mentality becomes an increasingly important human factor. This socio-technocratic world of the future has been labeled the Space Age, in which man is colonizing the planets and exploring into deep physical space, termed Noosphere* by Chardin, in which man is exploring also vast *intellectual* spaces.

By storming the vertical frontier of physical and mental space, he will make our society a multi-dimensional civilization instead of a two-dimensional civilization which is presently limited to the thin surface of this one small planet. However, the most significant factor of the coming technological age will be the new man-machine partnership in intellectual activities. The next decades will see the time come in which electronic machines become highly active in the intellectual activities of the world; and, as a consequence, the capacity for gathering and using information, that is, the overall brain power of the world, will increase manyfold.

CYBERNETICS

This aforementioned electronic brain-power age is already in progress. Most of the users and designers of today's machines are already concerned with the problem of how to utilize this powerful man-machine combination. It is important, however, to pause occasionally and take a long look ahead at how man can state testable hypotheses for this combination as well as to prescribe the process by which this combination is to operate. One important facet of this so-called Intelectronics Era,* then, is the matter of communication between man and the machine, and their mutual control, namely "cybernetics" in its relation to General Systems* theories.

The meaning of the term "cybernetics" is today somewhat different from that used when Wiener, McCulloch, Rosenblueth, Bigelow and others used the Greek word "Kybernetes," or helmsmen, to describe an automatic computer.

The term "cybernetics" was probably first used for communication control purposes by Ampére in 1824 and popularized by N. Wiener in 1948 in his book *Cybernetics,* and later in his revised edition in 1961. It has a number of definitions:

a)   "Cybernetics is the science which studies the communication and the processes of control in living organisms and machines." (Wiener, N., *Cybernetics,* 1948.)

b)   "Cybernetics is the science of the process of transmission, processing, and storage of information." (Sobolew, *Woprosy Psychology,* 1958.)

c)   "Theory of the interrelation of possible self-regulating dynamic systems and their partial systems." (Klaus, G., *Cybernetics and Philosophy.* Berlin, 1961.)

d)   "Cybernetics is restricted to research on processes which take place in automatic control systems, the flow of information therein, processing of this information, and the utilization of machines for these purposes." (Dietz, A., *Pedagogik,* 1963.)

I prefer this definition, which I first gave in 1966:
   "Cybernetics describes an intelligent activity or event which can be expressed in algorithms. Algorithms, in turn, refer to a system of instructions which describes unambiguously and accurately an interaction which is equivalent to a given type of flux of intelligence and a subsequent, controlled activity. The development of cybernetics aims, among other things, at the design and reproduction of functions which are peculiar to intelligent organisms."

A recent definition that I have advocated is simply:
"Cybernetics is the science of interactions."

This definition broadens the scope of cybernetics considerably. Although such a definition may transgress the claims of some ossified professors, who still cling desperately to the last straw of their "territoriality" before the inevitable change of the interdisciplinary approach to all of human knowledge, this definition passes any objective scrutiny. A brief argument goes something like this:

With the exception of the total energy content of the Universe, there is no static system. Even a chair on the floor is a dynamic system if we look on a molecular level to their interface under the influence of gravity. If we regard an individual entity, it, too, is in a dynamic interaction with its environment. Thus, there is interaction between atoms, people or galaxies. Everywhere one finds dynamism, and by definition there must be interaction. Interaction, on the other hand, is synonymous with a flow of information with a subsequent and inevitable control function. This is clearly congruent with the classical definition of cybernetics, and follows the laws of the information theories, also.

It might be also of value to define two subsciences of cybernetics: Bionics and Intelectronics.

Bionics is the science which deals with the transformation of organismic functions into electronic, mechanical, etc., analogs—in other words, the design and production of artificial organs and organisms, on one hand, and the design and production of artifacts modeled after organismic structures, on the other hand.

Intelectronics is essentially a bionic science which is restricted to the simulation of the brain or central nervous system and the design and production of artificial and suprahuman intelligence.

Cybernetics, being a truly interdisciplinary science, has an interface or overlap with many adjunct sciences, such as information theories, operations research, data processing, anatomy and physiology, psychodynamics, behavior engineering and various aspects of mathematics.

In connection with the intelligent machines, it is said that the speed and capacity of the input and output devices* have physical limitations second only to the great limitation of man's rate of information absorption. We need more efficient ways of bringing man's mind and the computer into proper communication. We shall find these ways in the coming decades.

The input/output problems, however, are not currently of prime importance to man-machine systems, because to attack these problems we need to know what the job of the combination should be, and we have so far not even scratched the surface in the overall use of machines in intellectual tasks. Today's ideas for the design of the machine that aids in intellectual tasks, and for hints for the means of communication between machine and man, are based on old ways of maintaining the logistics of the world, such as production, transportation, banking and government. So far, the electronic computing machines are only "fitting in" more than they are "revolutionizing" our way of operating.

If one wishes to talk about man-machine communication in the long-range future, it would be considered that the nature of this man-machine partnership in intellectual tasks will have a really substantial and basic effect on the way in which the physical operations of the world are organized and operated. The methodology in processing government, banking, transportation, production, merchandising, criminology, education, law, and medicine— all will have to be revised.

Professional and business intellectual activities have as yet hardly been changed. Even engineers use machines only to extend the computing capability of their minds, as they go about their tasks and routines as before.

In business, electronic machines are mostly repetitiously processing the large volumes of structured data, e.g., payrolls. Due to their efficiency, they are making possible a more economical operation, rather than effecting fundamental changes in information transferral procedures. Airlines may make reservations somewhat more automatically, and banks may handle their checks with less human interaction, but the basic approach to running airlines and banks has not yet been changed greatly by man-machine combination. The time and labor-saving business machines are only refined methods of an ancient process, as is the desk calculator or abacus for long-hand addition.

The impact of the man-machine of the future, which will be a much more highly intelligent and articulate combination than the man-machine combinations heretofore contemplated and implied, cannot even be compared with those currently available, which are capable only of high-capacity processing. This type we now class as "low intelligence" because their process is so readily understandable and easy to use. They relegate man to a linkage role in the problem-solving activity. It is certain that, years from today, research on intelligent man-machine combinations will have paid off. We will have available machines capable of heuristic* intellectual activities as yet only dimly conceived, that will be self-organizing and self-adaptive, and which most of mankind will be able to learn to use.

SOME ASPECTS OF AUTOMATION

It becomes necessary to look far ahead in man-machine communications because we are currently far behind in exploiting our understanding of significant steps which must precede the realization of a productive and desired plateau in the technological advances in this field. We must expect in the future the availability of an immense volume of knowledge which is instantly electronically accessible and which will involve every intellectual activity of all disciplines, cultural levels and political persuasions. There will be new operational methods of investigation and national schemes which will help man to influence the traditional practice of law, perhaps even the structure of law itself, as well as the making of new legislation; the research and practice of medicine will change, including even the goals of such efforts. Communication, transportation and production systems of material will change, and so will the behavior of people and their ideas. If this is true, then the theory and practice of cybernetic education becomes a very realistic problem today.

The first obvious question is, in what form and at what rate will man be using information in such an environment? The next problem is the nature of the messages between man and machine.

Furthermore, it has to be determined, in this close man-machine cooperation, what the work profile for the man will be and what is expected as the task for the machine. It can be assumed that the machine's role will be the handling of the large-volume, high-rate processing of information, the storing, correlating, comparing and sorting. The machine will also provide the speed and flexibility of interaction among those man-machine components of larger systems whose activities must be integrated over large distances and short times. In other words, we can assume that machines will be used for those tasks which are the least suitable for the human brain. The human partner will handle those "higher" intellectual mental activities that are less clear, that are heuristic, involving judgment, decision and the reaching of conclusions with severe consequences.

Under these conditions, man's capabilities intersect with the machine at a boundary which is not sharp or well defined. It is a transition between the high-capacity, definable level of the machine and the vague but sophisticated, complex level of the man. This type of intercourse will be the everyday, natural one in this future period, where children will grow up accustomed to it; hopefully, the adults will have prepared themselves for it.

The lawyer will be able to confer with the partial equivalent of thousands of other attorneys who have had similar cases by interrogating a data base which was carefully prepared and organized for this purpose. He will do this by beginning a dialogue with his intelectronic system, mentioning the essentials of his case and receiving, if called for, almost instantaneously, a display of pertinent facts, opinions, precedents and possible violations of laws or contests with the claims of others.

The physician will register the history and symptoms of his patient into a central computation facility, and could receive up-to-date statistical analyses, including suggestions for additional tests, treatment versus cure, prognosis or probabilities. The output of the computation center would also raise additional questions which the physician must answer to continue the dialogue with his "partner." This exchange between physician and machine could continue indefinitely (and be called research) if not terminated by practical considerations.

Business will be run in accordance with a continuously updated plan. Deviations could be automatically reported, analyzed and acted upon according to rules which are stored in magnetic memory banks. When the rules no longer cover the situations of previous experiences, then the information will be displayed to the human partners for phrasing new questions and initiating new routes to search.

The military will have large amounts of continuously revised information available about the political and military events from all over the world on a minute-to-minute basis. This is a necessary requirement in a civilization where unprepared nations can be destroyed in minutes. The mass of data will be continuously and instantaneously processed, compared, categorized and displayed. Furthermore, the decisions based on this display will be tested by running in the computer a continuous "war game" between the forces of friend and foe.

Traffic arteries in the sky and on the ground will be used with greater safety and yet higher capacity and speed, because man-machine combinations will accomplish the difficult job of keeping track of all parameters on a continuous flow basis by predicting consequences and computing directives for transmittal to the human operator. Even individual vehicles will have sensors, and will be able to compute higher order interactions, which man alone cannot do.

INTELLIGENT MACHINES

Man-machine communications in the future cannot be envisioned without imagining the parallel between past and future. There will exist new systems for handling intellectual functions that will have taken advantage of the possibility of matching man and machine as a combination for the performance of all types of intellectual tasks. For example, if before the industrial revolution we would have tried to visualize a world in which mountains would have to be moved by man, we could probably only recognize that man could not do so with his own hands or even with his horses or elephants helping him. We would have to virtually see the bulldozers at work to appreciate how man and machine might form a partnership to accomplish that mountain-moving task. We must not let limited imagination in looking ahead force us to narrow our conclusions.

Today, most of the communication between man and electronic computing devices is involved in transmitting and receiving exactly those kinds of data and performing those operations that we will have changed markedly by the year 2000. Looking ahead, we do not want man to take down information in longhand, then change it to punched cards and again to electrical signals; neither to pick up detailed numbers from the machine and examine them for reaching overall answers. Even in buying a car or a house, we will not want to have to write out a check and later have it read by a complex electronic device. It will be much more "human" to introduce a debit in our account and a credit to a seller's in electrical form. Therefore, most of the presently identified man-machine communications on the intellectual front will become machine-to-machine communications in the years to come. Millions of points on the surface of the earth will be in constant communication to maintain our physical operations at the accelerated, world-wide, integrated pace that will then exist, functioning mostly via satellites.

Certain segments of mankind in the future will have the capacity and the desire to deal only with big policy issues, not the details. Information of interest at this level of future human activity will be that which deviates from plans or which provides a challenge for creative thinking.

New sciences are in the making which will provide the tools for this aim. It is the basic idea in information theory that information need not be communicated unless there is some change from a previous understanding. Therefore, if this basic idea holds true, man will work towards a situation in which all of the important data which are needed can be gathered with a minimum of intervention by man. This information or peculiar aggregates of raw data should be assembled according to a plan for what should happen next as the consequence of the information. Man will be largely engaged with the formulation of plans and the selection of alternates where goals are not yet clear enough to be handled by the machine. But man will have to assume that the machines operate efficiently, that the right values reach the right points at the right time, because *they have been properly planned to do so.* Even such planning will have to be aided by the machine, because man would not be able to cope with all parameters. The machines will give man no information about any details of operations, and man will make no contribution to get into the act of lower order data processing, except insofar as the interim products of machine processing are interpreted by man to be inappropriate, i.e., change of values through time.

If the plan fails or if there are deviations from the plan, with no stored, predesignated action to cover that possibility, then the human partner will want to be advised, so that he can take proper action. Of course, after a period of time, his preferred action should be to alter or extend the plan. If this trend develops, man will work with combinations of machines towards higher and higher automated systems. The end goal is to eliminate the need for man to communicate with the machine on anything but the increasingly higher level of results, major deviations, or overall statistical analyses. As complexity increases, man will be more and more removed from the physical aspects of the partnership with the machine. Man may become disinterested and eventually even incapable of dealing with more than one or two significant figures. Man will be looking at a display of overall effects, asking for gross impressions that will stimulate creative thinking of new interrelationships, rules and structure, searching for basic trends that will show weaknesses in the existing man-machine partnership in problem-solving processes.

There is a great deal of research going on in this field, at least along theoretical and fundamental lines, by the engineers, physical and biological scientists, and by psychologists as well. Some of the research deals with the comprehension of the human mind as a physical machine. The expectation is that, on one hand, knowing the networks and the processes in the organization of man's ten billion neurons* will yield beneficial consequences in neurology and psychology. On the other hand, it will teach us fundamentals applicable to machines with better components.

Unfortunately, little work is in progress which investigates man and machine as a combination for problem solving; the mechanics of such solution processes are very involved, but certain types of problems only man-machine combinations will be able to handle.

When such intelligent machines are available, they will assume part of the human brain activities. They will not only eliminate some of the current man-machine communication by emphasizing the communication between machines, but also the communication in which man is involved will be changed because man will have to talk to this more intelligent machine that shares with him some of the more subtle thinking tasks that he now handles alone. It is not easy, however, to envision how man will talk to his new partner. Perhaps it will be largely in terms of goals, or perhaps in a form of dialogue concerning projected goals or on-line prediction, since the future is never perfectly predictable and the environment will at no time be completely defined.

Consider that the basic factual information is available to and through the machines in the world of the future. We are presumably able to design these more intelligent machines because we are able to describe increasingly complex processes that we should like to have applied to basic facts. Thus, we need to add to the machine's knowledge only our goals and to get back from the machine only its answers, or its questions as to our goals. If, at any rate, the machines need more of the pertinent data, then we would arrange to connect it to the proper sources of the facts and not allow ourselves to act as go-betweens.

To illustrate this, let us imagine an industrial organization which is operating with highly optimized plans. The planks of the organizational platform take into account the fluctuating sales and market technological breakthroughs, stockholders' opinions, variations in the quality of the raw materials furnished, even unpredictable conditions in the weather or politics. Supposedly, we shall be able to state what end results we wish to achieve. Also, we are aware of the main factors that may influence the results, and all the facts are available which relate to those very issues. Then we can imagine the design and construction of devices which can provide alternatives that are the equivalent of what the human mind would have arrived at, given enough time and all of the same basic data and logical rules. Notice that in the face of uncertainty the decision maker still has to decide by assigning *limited* resources to a project in the *hope* of a payoff.

There is, however, an additional echelon of information that should be allowed to have some influence on the analyses and the decisions that we are trying to reach. These are the physically or mathematically less tangible data which the human psyche utilizes quite readily, although sometimes in a somewhat irrational way. For example, what could be the specific effect on, let us say, linear programming* of anything we read in the newspaper? The machine could, of course, read the newspaper as well. But what will this brilliant machine make of the news it sees there? How should the enormously broad spectrum of events pictured in a newscast be interpreted by the machine? One answer is that it should do exactly what the human mind does. Now, how does the mind of a chief executive of an industrial concern influence his operations as he reads and interprets the news? How does the world picture influence his judgment during the day? What he does is probably not what we desire to have the machine do. Why duplicate the human brain in its present state of confusion as to the relationship between the enormous number of qualitative, diverse factors outside and the chief issues of the business? It is doubtful that, even if we could, we should produce machines that are complete copies of the human brain and its capabilities. We have already two billion such brains, and their further "production" is not difficult. No skilled labor is necessary to manufacture them, and the labor unions will be satisfied because everyone loves the job!

Communication in a higher organism, including man, involves the ability to originate signals with his body and receive them with his sense organs. As tools for communication, the language, or set of symbols, is used for any environment, but these tools will have to change. In a cybernetic age, in an age of man-machine partnerships in intellectual activities, a new language, a new set of symbols, is needed; and it will come eventually on a world-wide basis.

Ordinary, natural language of the past, spoken or written, is not favored by the machine. It does not suit very well the extending of human communication. It will influence the spoken and written language of our everyday, man-to-man communications. As man-machine communications become common routine and everybody's business, this language becomes the "natural" one to use. At the beginning, while the vocabulary is both restricted and precise, the origin of the language is not important. It is relatively easy for such language to be international, just as are, e.g., binary digits.* As time goes on, this factual, machine-adapted language has at least as good a chance of spreading over the world as any spoken language previously suggested. For the physical

operations of the world, it is a far stronger candidate for
world-wide standardization than universal language proposals of
the past, such as Esperanto, Ido, etc., that were invented before
the machine partner had a vote.

The universal language for machine and man for the future,
that will have a controlling influence on communications, should
consider a number of novel features. One of these is the
elimination of the decimal number system and its replacement by
the binary system, or a more appropriate system which is better
suited for electronic switching systems of computers. This would
not be more difficult than the abolition of the antiquated English
measuring system. The language of the future will be characterized
by uniform sentence structure, with the subject always preceding
the predicate noun or verb, and with no participle clauses dangling
like this one.

It can be expected that standard color codes will evolve as
additional symbols to convey universal meanings in visual display
of information. Perhaps there will be standardized coding of
three-dimensional displays, all in the interest of improving the bit
rate of transmission to the human mind through one's eyes.
Similarly, standard rhythmical acoustic patterns will come to have
special meanings. Even acoustic signals which can be easily
originated by man either through spoken words, finger-snaps, or
taps, might be used with considerable efficiency. When coupled
with the variety of sounds which can be originated by electrical
means, the man-machine combination of the future has an almost
unlimited capacity for communicating between man and machines. The limited capacity of the human brain to utilize more
than about 40 bits per second information flux* for decision
making prompted the present writer to design the Pragmatoscope.* There is a spatio-temporal bottleneck in the data
processing of the brain. Yet, in certain operations, fast human
decisions are imperative, and may be based on the need of an
information flux of many hundred bits per second. If they are
forced upon the mind in the form of a visual display of symbols,
the brain will rationalize and, in congruence with the Gestalt
theory,* will group these symbols into assemblies or units of many
symbols to reduce their numbers to an acceptable and meaningful
level. Unfortunately, the value of the individual symbol within the

group is lost or is made less accessible for decision making.

The preceding discussion may suggest at first that the big problem of man-machine communications in the age ahead is for man to communicate all of the facts and numbers into the machine. The latter then can go to work on the data. Consequently, man will be able to understand quickly the new numbers or facts that the machine turns up. This is, however, if not wrong, at least too narrow a look at the problem.

The more available the machines become to do the high-capacity data processing in partnership with man, the more efficient partners the machines will become to do higher and higher level intellectual tasks. Because only the goals and criteria are to be furnished, it is very likely that, with the aid of the machine partner, we will much improve the clarity of these goals. One of our problems today in reading the newspaper and interpreting it in relation to our life's work is that we are lost in a tremendous sea of unprocessed data, unconfirmed data, and not-well-understood data.

The world of the future should be one in which it will be possible to have more reliable and properly processed facts on the entire human situation, or on any issue that is worthy of further thought. We shall be in less doubt as to what people think as they make statements, because it should be possible with improved communications to get more precise facts and report them accurately in the appropriate amount at the highest attainable level of credibility. We shall not have to debate so much the merits of a proposed package of additional legislation because we will be able to predict the consequences of the new legislation by assuming that it has actually existed over the past few years and then by analyzing the mass of quantitative and qualitative data covering those aspects of life to which this law would apply. Or, in a business, the management will be able to know the inventories, the market, the state of the profit potential and many external factors, so that over a period of time relationships will become clearer between decisions and their consequences.

Predictions of the man-machine combination, in utilizing Markov-chain-type* probabilistic mathematical operations, with the available mass of data, will simplify and stabilize our now emotion-packed public life. Such man-machine combinations will successfully eliminate controversies based on the disbelief of the opponent's data and the misinterpretation of his statements.

It would appear, then, that man-machine communications in the future will gradually be dominated more and more by the assignment of the detail to the machine partner, which will grow in versatility as well as in capacity and overall intelligence. Increasingly, man will concentrate on that part of intellectual activity where there is a lack of clarity as to goals, as to facts, and as to what rules of logic or illogic we choose to apply. Man-machine communications will grow up in an environment in which man is pushed to being more scientific, more logical, more consistent and more factual in his approach to every intellectual task. As he increases his intellectual stature, with the aid of his machine, he transfers the clear activities and the understood mental processes to the machine and thus can attack always the next layer of vagueness and confusion.

Man may become a polymorphic switch* in the man-machine system, and he will be needed in the network only to call out guiding suggestions, receiving general indications on the basis of which his suggestions may be modified. Below this level he will find the machines busy with the maze of detail about which we shall care increasingly less. In the purely physical operations of the world, to which details apply, we shall be satisfied with considerable automation.

So far, we have dealt mostly with one of the most important aspects of a cybernetic world, namely, *communication.* It is equally important to mention the developments in *control.*

Communication and amassing of information are performed by the conscious mind as a tool in the process of controlling organismic activities. In ultimate analysis, one can easily see that life, the establishment of an optimum niche and self preservation, is based to a great extent on the social activities of man. In this endeavor, man utilizes information mostly for decision making with subsequent transfer of psychomotor* functions into control activities to shape his external environment.

At the same rate as future deployment of information will change fundamentally, the means of communication and also methods of control functions will undergo basic transformation. Here again, today's technology has already outraced human bodily capabilities, and a new close partnership is developing presently between man and machine, not only by the machine assisting in overcoming physical afflictions, but also by extending man's inherent physical capabilities to undreamed levels.

In the past, the man-machine interface in control mechanisms was restricted to the manipulation of knobs, dials, etc., with the human extremities, which constitute a most bothersome bottleneck encountered in sub-miniaturization of electronic devices. As long as the machine could be designed around the capacity of the human body, only minor problems had to be solved. But the requirements of high performance equipment, designed by man for man's progressive living pattern, exceeds the anthropometric* and biodynamic* limits of the average man. Therefore, machines had to be designed which extended the human capacity in the sense of mechanical and steady state equipment.

This need laid the foundation for the science of Bionics. Through Bionics, the shortcomings of the human organism, which were brought about and shaped by environmental stresses and subsequent evolution, will be reduced. Thus, it is envisioned that many control functions which cannot and should not be automated for error-correcting reasons will be performed by man without much fatigue and in good time due to the application of bionic devices.

The implanting of bionic devices into the body for the enhancement of its function does not seem to alter essentially the nature of the organism. It is hoped, although on an emotional basis, that in the far future, when the number of electromechanical implants or exchange of organs becomes very high, man will not lose his identity. However, such desire may be nothing else but atavistic sentiment.

At any rate, we are racing into a greatly and basically different world in which we should and must live in relative harmony. And the only means by which this can be achieved is through education.

Education is becoming the most important tool for survival because it establishes the optimized niche for man, thus contributing to his happiness. Happiness, in turn, is not only the main goal of man, but also an important factor for his operational integrity.

EDUCATION AT A CROSSROAD

The most striking symptom of this new area is that real progress can be brought about only by interdisciplinary work producing multidisciplinary ideas within a systems frame of reference. The time has passed when comparative vertebrate anatomy can be taught for that discipline's sake alone. No one denies, of course, that the promotion of the state-of-the-art in this nature-mosaic is important, and some scientists will find it their pleasure to devote their time to such tasks. But major steps in general human progress will come about only from the efforts of men who regard individual disciplines as *pars pro toto.* * All human endeavors are to be regarded as a single system of innumerable sub-systems and interrelated dynamic components.

One of the most significant innovations in pedagogical methodology will be to use the human brain in entirely different dimensions from those attempted by the schools of today. At present, the virtue of learning is synonymous with loading the memory with the largest possible number of facts. Almost every effort in teacher training, audio-visual aids, teaching machine construction and examination objectives is directed mainly toward amassing stored raw data.

Unfortunately, the human memory is not only limited as to theoretical capacity, but it has many shortcomings which make it quite inadequate to handle the information content of even one modern discipline, not to mention the data from all other disciplines which may have interactions with the one in question.

Contrary to machine memories, often important data which are prominently placed in the human memory matrix* are not instantaneously accessible; if not used frequently, they will become faulty or fade away completely. On the other hand, outdated, unimportant, or even undesired data often cannot be erased from the memory; thus, they will, by unintended reson-ance-recall, termed "association," unduly influence judgment.

A further shortcoming of the human memory is that its acceptance of information depends on the variable nature of a series of narrow band-pass filters* called "intelligence quotient," "indoctrination," "emotional makeup," etc. Furthermore, the accepted data are assessed for quite subjective values and deposited accordingly in priority levels. Therefore, in a man-to-man communication, the same data can have different meanings, thus making a team effort in problem solving very unreliable. This circumstance also excludes the possibility that complex interdisciplinary problems, requiring an information density of many human memory capacities, could be solved efficiently by a team of persons who are educated in the traditional way.

In the man-machine age of tomorrow, however, most of the data will be deposited with the objectivity of the machine. Its memory capacity will be virtually unlimited, and needed information will be available with predetermined value rules by speedy scanning or from instantaneously accessible function banks.*

In the relatively near future, man will operate these machines to extract the necessary data for goal-directed activities, which he will use, or misuse, by skewing their values by intangible factors, such as likes or dislikes. Later, however, possibly in the early 22nd Century, the human mind will be directly coupled with a data-processing device. The latter, in turn, has access to the memory bank of the total human knowledge and human judgment; thus, the formulating of pertinent questions will be more meaningful and less dependent upon the variability of individual human personalities who are in the ocean of biological spread.*

In the past 3000 years, education has been successful in preparing those who were interested in knowledge. Knowledge, however, was and still is synonymous with quantity or inventory of stored data. A highly qualified specialist of the future will not only be a plant taxonomist who knows the name and some characteristics of 200,000 plants, an astrophysicist who can compute the orbital characteristics of a celestial body, or an "expert" who did some experiments with slime molds, but also the man who can formulate the questions and detect the problems which require solution for the welfare of an individual or the efficiency of a community. This trend does not exclude, of course, the virtue of the advancement of the sciences, *l' art pour l' art.* *

This era seems far in the future, yet the trend in data utilization is already changing today. Therefore, educators must accommodate the new trend in the meaning of knowledge, and must educate people primarily in the systems approach, data retrieval and problem solving, rather than in enjoying a glorious inventory of data in the mind, which a primitive machine or even the obsolete invention of Gutenberg, the folded book, can handle much better.

The future pedagogy will have to teach children to read, because the visual information displays with meaningful symbology are very efficient tools of communication. But writing can begin to be de-emphasized, because already today's children can become highly efficient in typing (and they like it much better than longhand); and the voicerecorder and other voice transcribing devices which are on the drawing board or in the R & D phase will make the time-consuming and tedious writing with the hand a ridiculous effort.

There is little question that the time is overdue for a significant revision of our ossified educational processes. If we want education to fulfill its purpose of preparing this generation for problems of future decades and current unresolved problems, long-range plans must be started today to tailor education to tomorrow's pattern of our technocratic society.

Learning is a self-assumed task with self-imposed goals. Learning can be thought of as combining the storage of primarily analytical information with some synthetic concept images. Here, the intrinsic and extrinsic environments are merely temporal factors—every man with average intelligence can learn anything, provided he is familiar with the nomenclature of the subject matter, is given unlimited time, and has defined goals. It is presupposed, of course, that the individual has the desire to learn and has the necessary patience.

Teaching, on the other hand, is a much more difficult problem, because it involves the intricacies of communication between two or more humans. The problems are, among many others, the estimates of the learner's ability, the timing of information transmissions, the error correction of basic analytical data, goals, nomenclature, etc., and, last, but not least, the personality interactions, with feedback loops between teacher and student.

Instruction, which refers to the useful interaction between teacher and student, must have a close link to the intricacies of Nature or to the requirements of human labor or life in general.

This statement is in full harmony also with the instruction of the humanities and the arts. Obviously, education is not only the cognition of reality and scientific foresight, but also the medium for the conscious influence of all objective processes of man in the interest of his intellectual betterment and the improvement of his society.

The school, or perhaps more vividly referred to as pedagogical laboratories, of the future will be built so that the information is introduced, processed and presented by child-machine intelectronic components. A classroom, which is unlikely to exist much longer in its present form, can be regarded as a system of similar components. In such a system, the material is automatically varied in its speed and density, while presented in accordance with the continuously tested and recorded ability of the student to understand. Educational planning will be based in part on statistical averages of results which can be compared semi-automatically against the estimates, the goals, and the techniques used. All this points to a *revolution* of education if it comes upon us fast, and a more desirable *evolution* only if we prepare for it.

Today's pedagogical methods are quite literally *ancient*. It is expected that in the intelectronic age of tomorrow, the so far unknown scientific laws of pedagogy will be detected, which will make knowledge a more easily accessible goal.

Cybernetics will aid education in many ways, such as:

a. It will help to automate the retrieval and storage of data.
b. It will determine the volume and content of educational need for society, production, science and the national interest.
c. It will help in well-substantiated planning and locating of the network and type of schools, etc.

Cybernetics is particularly suitable to study the improvements of pedagogical techniques.

In spite of its complexity, pedagogy will lend itself well to a mathematical approach as soon as its basic laws are discovered. There are, of course, a number of difficult steps which must be mastered first, such as defining the frame of pedagogy as a unified system, the coding and value assessment of the different disciplines as sub-systems, the quantification of human intelligence, the noise factors in education, etc.

The need to reveal the laws of pedagogy is most important because the mass of instructional material and the mass of students have downgraded the previously enviable profession of teaching. Pedagogy must become a science in order to fulfill its purpose under the present socio-economic world pattern. We do not have time any longer to let talented instructors become good teachers by pleasantly comfortable decades of empirical-practical experience.

The scientific recognition and utilization of pedagogical laws will be immeasurably more efficient than the Socratian type of instruction.* Everyone who is an educator at heart feels nostalgic about the vanishing "good old" teaching art, where the transmittal of personality traits from the "big old man" to the eager young student was emphasized as strongly as "Knowledge" of the discipline. Time was an independent variable.

Today, time has become, by necessity, a function of the quantity of information, whereby the descriptive phase of pedagogy is being replaced by exact experimentation and by statistical-mathematical methods.

The greatest challenge which faces future educators in a democratic system is to preserve and foster human individuality in spite of mechanistic pedagogical methods. We feel that cybernetics can aid this effort. The proper design of information channels and the careful insertion of human variables into the system dynamics may enhance humanism, which is lost by applying antiquated techniques to an overloaded (in channel permeability) and underpowered (in capability) open-loop system.*

Cybernetic pedagogy will, in its analytical phase, penetrate deep into the essentials of teaching; then, in its synthetic phase, will exactly calculate the expected results, and will be able to formulate prognoses for the development of processes. This will, no doubt, eliminate the often irreversible errors and consequent failures in present day teaching.

In the discussion between teacher and pupil, where information is exchanged, education requires that the information should be properly coded to make it suitable for transmission. The transmission should be reliable and fast, which requires the establishment of transmission channels with the proper band widths and permeability. This indicates an improved language, as long as telepathy is not available. The received information must be decoded to make it meaningful and available for value assessment. At this point, a feedback loop is required from the pupil to the teacher and, after error correction, the information is channeled into storage, but not before recoding it to fit the memory requirements, a process which necessitates a new application of mnemotechnique.*

It is obvious that all these steps are the essentials also of automatic control systems to which cybernetics is applied so successfully. It can be expected that similar benefits will occur in its application to pedagogy. At this point, it should be mentioned that the principles of algorithms* will play an important part in the field of investigation of teaching methods.

In approaching problems of pedagogy from the cybernetic point of view, it is presupposed that all processes of reality follow certain general laws which should be found also in teaching. Only then can pedagogic factors be clearly understood and thoroughly evaluated. The great difficulty in pedagogic research arises from the fact that all the complex interactions between teacher, pupil and environment must be taken into consideration.

There are a large number of channels used for information transmittal: words, gestures, pictures, text, etc. A good teacher intuitively encourages the student to raise many-sided questions to gain information through an optimum number of channels and the greatest possible frequency of confrontation.

Most useful assistance can be obtained from cybernetics in the study of "noise" in the network. This refers to those factors in instruction which interfere with the speed and fidelity of information transmission. Also, many aspects of the information theories can be applied to teaching. For instance:

"The reliability and quality of information transmission decreases with the speed of transmission," or

"The speed of transmission of information by a given channel system has a maximum. If this maximum is reached, there is no further possibility for increase," etc.

The chief difficulty in applying cybernetics to pedagogy lies in the fact that cybernetics is primarily a statistical science based on probabilities and the cyclic forms of mathematics.

In the dawn of the intelectronics age, information and the value of knowledge are growing into a dimension which can no longer be obtained, comprehended and stored by the methods of yesteryear. Even if the less pertinent details are eliminated from the "need to know," the general structure of life and society is becoming so complex that only a revolutionary new system of education can provide man with the tools for maintaining his efficiency in society and thus ensuring his happiness. In this new system, the elementary and secondary school teachers will assume new stature.

In the future, the college professor who spends his lifetime interested only in the synthesis of the yellow heterocyclic azo dyes, or the fascinating story of the sexual reproduction of slime mold (mycomycetae), will be regarded only as a producer of important, sometimes very important and even useful raw data. In contrast, the elementary and secondary teacher will have to have a profound knowledge not only of the principles of all sciences, including those of social aspects, as well as the humanities, but must also be a cybernetician with a good working knowledge of computer technology and information theories.

This, unfortunately, will exclude the "lil old lady" or the retired officer from supplementing their meager (or not so meager) pension with the easily accessible teacher certificate. It is felt fair to emphasize here, however, that many of these "supplement" teachers are doing a much better job in today's type of education than many original pros, who started off in a teachers' college because admittedly it required less effort and brain power for graduation, or because the candidate was unable to cope with the mastery of the 60 credit hours of more or less useful, highly specialized courses in his carefully (?) chosen major.

The ne / type of elementary or early secondary teacher will enjoy high esteem due to his superior background. The state will demand supericr training of youngsters who are in their ideal state of information in.print. Also, parents will bear pressure on the school system to provide their children with the most efficient pedagogical techniques, which will ensure rapid mental growth even before all "necessary" facts have been memorized.

One will find that the present avenue, namely, the method to force upon the mind of the child a set of facts without which the more general concepts of systems cannot be taught, is not the only road to Rome. To teach general principles in the early grade schools and let the students pick up the detailed information as they go will be a much better form in the future. If some of the facts are frequently used, the student will learn them automatically, and those facts which he does not need frequently can be stored much better by a well designed data processor than by his brain. From the processor they can be extracted by the flip of a finger *today,* which will display the required information at the command of a thought *tomorrow,* and which will deliver the answer to a question directly into the human brain the *day after tomorrow.*

The new education will be based on results obtained by advanced teaching machines, which will automatically establish a student's aptitude, maturity, background information, dexterity in handling experiments and even personality profile.

On the basis of this information, the coupled computer, which is specially designed and programmed, will assign the student to the best available teacher—who is a specialist in conceptual instruction of a certain "readiness" level of the student.

The efficiency of such a teacher will be incomparably greater than that of today's teachers, because he will work with a homogeneous group. The age of his pupils may vary greatly, but their "teachability" will be almost identical. Everybody who has taught in school will appreciate this.

After the general system approach of the material, learned with the aid of the teaching machine, is well covered, the student will be sent to another teaching machine. As soon as the student has absorbed the material, which will be so programmed that it is based on the previous experience and learning, a machine will again assign the student to a teacher. It is quite likely that this second group will not be identical with the group which has passed the instruction of the first teacher, because of differences in intelligence and motivation.

There will be, of course, no grades or examination, because, through its manifold feedback system, the machine will evaluate the student's degree of education; and the topics covered by the teacher are the basis of the next level of machine instruction. Furthermore, as indicated before, the machine measures the readiness of the student; thus, the human material which will emerge from institutes of higher learning will be of *predictable quality*. This will be invaluable for the industry or other enterprises which are in need of competent employees, because today's MS or PhD degrees are of very low fidelity as a tool to ascertain the efficiency, ingenuity, diligence, team compatibility, etc., of the proud bearer of a shingle.

It is known that it takes courage to look ahead and accept the future, because it is incongruent with our experience. This is a critical age, in which the continuing progress of mankind is at stake. As in mythology, where Prometheus brought the fire to Earth and with it provided superiority for mankind, today intelligent machines may help to conquer not only the universe, but also ourselves.

2.

CYBERNETIC PLURALISM

Some Philosophical Aspects of Cybernetics

It is "old hat" with the present writer to search for a unified philosophical frame which, on one hand encompasses all animate and inanimate matter of the universe and, on the other hand, gives an emotionally more satisfying platform than does a pure Haeckelian monism.*

Severe rebuttal for the term "emotional" is expected but, unscientific as it may sound, it is felt that philosophies are essentially anthropocentric.* Although it may seem at first illogical, truth, even logical truth, is relative. It is relative to the socio-cultural trends under which the determiner of the truth lives. Hereby no comparatively small niches or environments, even of the size of a country, are in question. Of course, many do not subscribe to anthropocentric teleology.* However, it is highly probable that the personality of a sane, adult human, in his behavioral and spiritual expression, is inescapably subject to the influence of his environment, and thus to his socio-cultural milieu.

One would not doubt that details, such as fundamentals of mathematics, the laws of motion, thermodynamics, or maybe even cosmology, can be treated without personality bias. But in those cases where correlates of higher order occur in which speculation

29

of an analytical type leaves the terrain of pure data-processing and enters into the realm of supra system comprehension, the speculator obviously cannot jump out of his skin; he must be satisfied to accomplish his tasks within the limitations of his mind. In turn, his mind is subject to vectors set by his environment.

This will explain and justify the statement that today a philosophical approach to the post-cybernetic world is a natural consequence of the advances which are being made by the sciences during the second half of this century.

There seem to be two essential factors which may, as soon as they become "reality" in the human sense, contribute to a new philosophy. These two factors are the possibility of intelligent extra-terrestrial life and the radical change in meaning of the semantic term "machine."

It can be argued that a philosophical adaptation to a problem, which inevitably will arise by the detection of intelligent extra-terrestrial life, would be better founded if and when such life has been detected.

On the other hand, it can be considered a safety precaution to deal with the matter beforehand in order to avoid or dampen the shock when it occurs. And should it never occur, the effort can be written off as mental exercise, which in itself is a delightful pastime.

The second item mentioned, concerning the changes in the meaning of the concept "machine," hinges, of course, on communication rather than on pure semantics. Even this latter statement is dependent upon the basic theories of communication if we go beyond the mere dictionary definition.

To communicate thoughts one is compelled to use now and in this country the ordinary English instead of thought transfer—extrasensory perception (ESP)—or at least a meta-language which has a higher fidelity for the transmission of the information content of the needed concepts. Operational ESP is not yet here in spite of the contract awards which the government has drawn up for research of this type. A useful meta-language is at least 50 years away, although feverish efforts are being made in many quarters.

Before one engages in the experiment of laying down a

foundation for a new philosophy, it will be necessary to examine critically the essential terms which may be required.

TOWARD A NEW PHILOSOPHY

One of the most perplexing and complicated aspects of information transmission is linguistic. The mechanism of formation of words and the structuring of sets of character symbols for the expression and transmission of mental concepts is still obscure. Even simple but meaningful sentences, if analyzed, lose much of their rigor and become quite vague as to information content.

To demonstrate this, let us choose the phrase, "the effects of extra-terrestrial life." The word "effect" has an immense information content if all of its ramifications are revealed. First of all, it implies causality, which in itself has been challenged recently. The main shortcoming of this word in the connotation of the sentence above is that it is dimensionless; it does not possess any spatio-temporal constraints; nor can it be quantified in other coordinate systems.

Therefore, in the present context, let us use the word "effect" very loosely, leaving room for a latitude in interpretation. In this way one will avoid the accusation of engaging in an unscientific approach.

The next term to which attention should be paid is "extra-terrestrial." Now this term, one would think, does not contain more than perhaps a few dozen bits of information. Therefore, it provides less opportunity for sowing confusion. Everything which is not in the realm of Terra is extra-terrestrial. And just what is the extent of this realm? Is it the "globe" which we call the earth? (By satellite research* we have learned that the earth is somewhat pear-shaped.) But would you not agree that the atmosphere is also part of the realm of Terra? How about the magnetic field or the gravitational field of the earth? Is this, too, within the realm of Terra? Without even engaging in the intricacies of the general theory of relativity or in other unified field theories, the astronauts provided verification that the realm of Terra covers an enormous amount of space. Some reader may invoke the inverse square law at this point and charge this chapter with "splitting hairs." Therefore, let us postulate that beyond the moon the realm is too weak to be considered. This is the type of convenient reasoning which is effectively used by philosophers, politicians, and psychiatrists. Thus, should we find a living organism between here and the moon, by definition it cannot be considered as extra-terrestrial. If you do not like this statement, then we can set the limit of the upper atmosphere at, let us say, 200,000 feet altitude. Or, if even this is more "extra" than "terrestrial" for the reader, then let us try once more. Extra-terrestrial refers to an object which originates more than 100,000 miles away from Earth. How about a human colony on Mars? Are the human children born on Mars "extra-terrestrial"?

If the reader reexamines what has just been said, he will find that one is not just juggling with words but fighting a battle for universal comprehension, the lack of which, in large measure, can be blamed for wars and racial and political controversies.

Let us then continue with our list of words basic to the present context and try to provide an appropriate meaning for the term "life." In trying to define "life" there seem to be three convenient approaches: 1) to contrast life with death, 2) to contrast animate versus inanimate, and 3) to arbitrarily accept one of the many definitions offered by scientists or philosophers. To contrast life with death is not a profitable approach because, in a way, it can be included in the discussion of animate versus inanimate. Furthermore, to quote from the *Ethics* of Spinoza "there is nothing over which a free man ponders less than death, his wisdom is to meditate not on death but life . . ."

However, there is one point of interest which can be used later for our deliberations. Regarding complex metazoic* organisms such as animals or man, even the medical sciences do not agree upon a clear definition for the concept of "death." It is well known that after the heartbeat and respiration have ceased, the whiskers of a "dead man" will continue to grow; after the head of an animal is removed, it is considered "dead" by everyone, yet there remain many organs in its body which function fully for a considerable length of time. A piece of tissue from a chicken's heart or some other animal or plant, when removed from the organism, can live in a proper environment almost indefinitely. Is such excised heart or brain tissue, recognizing that these organs are the symbolic locations of virtue, alive? Does a tissue culture of human brain contain any part of a "soul," to use this term temporarily? Most readers would say, "No." Students of cybernetics would say that the condition in which the "soul" can exist is in the complete system of the biological sub-entities which we call "man." Let us try to punch a hole into this "systems approach." Let us assume that we have a living man and we cut him into pieces and are able to keep these pieces alive *in vitro,** with all cells functioning and metabolizing in the same way as in the body. Now, let us put all of these functioning parts of the living man into one tissue culture chamber. Does this cabinet contain a "soul"? Is it governed by the same transcendental organization which is labeled with fancy names? Such terms as the biological force or entelechia, as defined by Driesch,* or other terms we might choose, are words without real meaning, but they have enabled the scientists to communicate and describe a syndrome for which they had no better theoretical approach. However, recently the basic and applied biological sciences have explained in clear language and beyond any reasonable doubt the biophysical and biochemical causes, consequences and interrelationships of many of the mysterious phenomena of life. Eventually, in such cases, the boundaries for entelechia had to be shifted. They had to be shifted again and again, *pari passu,** in harmony with the new biological discoveries. So the biologists and their running mates, the biochemists and biophysicists, dug deeper and deeper into the manifoldness and multiplicity of biological structure. In consequence, there was more and more material to be absorbed and comprehended. To master even a subsidiary science today requires an exceptional brain with encyclopedic talents. Yet there seems to be a heritage from our early ancestors—the longing and searching for universal, all-embracing knowledge. A true overall picture, however, can be gained only if it is based on the proper foundation of scientific detail. Such detail might or might not reveal certain regularities, the so-called physical laws, which will simplify somewhat the chaotic abundance of facts.

To determine whether an organism is living or not is not always easy. For instance, a bacterium or a seed will not show any of the characteristics of life unless the bacterium is brought under favorable conditions and is reproduced or, in the case of the seed it is allowed to germinate. This might take as much time as two years, as e.g., in the case of the iris.

As a second approach to defining life, let me adopt a definition offered by certain distinguished thinkers. The great majority of these definitions, however, are far too general. Exceptions can be found to most of them and they cannot answer exactly the question as to whether a given body is living or dead. William Roux postulates that a body is living if it shows the following characteristics: metabolism, growth, irritability, reproduction, and inheritance. Still more vague are the following definitions:

"Life exists wherever there is evidence of a certain instability." (Dubois-Raymond)

"Life is present wherever the peculiar phenomenon of movement, which characterizes life, exists." (Haeckel)

"Life is a continuous adaptation to internal and external conditions." (Spencer)

"Living bodies are capable of controlling automatically those stores of energy which are necessary for the stationary maintenance of their state." (Ostwald)

None of these definitions can, however, help to decide in every respect, whether a cell is living or dead.

Let me show, however, that, as is the case with so many statements, there are exceptions even here. If we place yeast cells in a dilute methylene blue solution, the dead cells will stain blue; the live ones will not. And, of course, we have the biochemical explanation for this phenomenon.

The definition and the criteria of "intelligence" have not yet been discussed, not because the task is so formidable but because it is rather space consuming and the well explored topic of a number of philosophers. There are even more difficulties in trying to predict the definition of life in a super-human intellect.

In approaching the living microcosmos as a target to localize the elementary unit of life, one is faced with many difficulties, and there is little or no chance of overcoming them completely.

There are two roads open to this approach. One is through the study of chromosomes; the other leads into the field of viruses and enzymes.

The hereditary mechanism could be located in parts of the cell nucleus. It could be shown beyond doubt that the genes, which are built in chain-like chromosomes, are responsible for most of the hereditary transmission of physical and psychical characteristics. Each of these genes is performing complex functions far beyond our intellectual capacity to structure in all their interrelationships. It can be assumed that even if the biological sciences should advance to a degree where the multitudiness of the physical and chemical reactions in the genes is understood, there will still remain phenomena which require an entirely different approach.

Science has gone so far as to be able to extract certain constituents of the nucleus. Direct operations on living cell nuclei and chromosomes are already in progress, and biochemists working on the molecular level of life have separated nucleoproteins which are highly important parts of the intimate machinery of the genes. It is of great significance that one of the most important compounds in the chemical reactions of genes, namely, deoxyribo nucleic acids (DNA), are present in an amount of about 10^{-13} oz. per cell. (Ten billion cells contain one ounce of DNA.) This means that the quantity of DNA, having a fairly high molecular weight, approaches the level where a very few, or even a single molecule, can be responsible for actions typical of living matter.

Classical genetics and cytology have gone about as far as this in explaining the gene. It still remains for scientists to complete the analysis and discover the irreducible unit of living structure.

Nobody would deny that uni-cellular organisms are living creatures, and biology accepts the cell in general as the unit of living matter. Science could demonstrate that this is not true of all parts of the cell, but that primarily the nucleus is the true site of life. It could be shown, furthermore, that parts of the nucleus have significantly greater importance for the maintenance of life than others. Since we can definitely state that the cell wall or certain proteins in the cytoplasm are not carrying the characteristics of life, can we then call nuclear bodies such as mitochondria, Golgi-bodies, microsomes, etc., alive? Or, can we go so far as to say that the smallest units in which life is manifest are molecules of the nucleoproteids or the enzymes?

It is beyond doubt that viruses can be considered as living uni-cellular organisms. The size of these viruses is in the neighborhood of one-millionth of an inch. This organism is still large enough to perform a wide variety of phenomena of life, and it is certain that a relatively large part of it acts only as a protective cover or the vehicle for the biologically more significant structural units. In the active ingredients of the genes, which are known to have a very high molecular weight, we have arrived again in the neighborhood of the dimension of single molecules.

Biochemists could trace life down to them. But the picture is still more confusing, because the same biochemists have succeeded in isolating some of the same enzymes in crystalline form and DNA in the form of a white amorphous powder. Both are inanimate and behave as it is expected from any organic compound on the shelf of a laboratory.

Now to go briefly beyond the human intellect to define life. An important consideration in assessing super-human intellects is our capability of comprehension. How can the impact of a "factor" be analyzed if we cannot and will *never* be able to comprehend it? The time factor "never" is not used as a figure of speech, but as a determinator. Thus, it does not mean that it is a function of our knowledge as would have been a forecast fifty years ago stating that man would *never* be able to fly faster than sound. For instance, if there were a world with two-dimensional intelligent creatures on it, they would have only the sense for the directions of left and right and forwards and backwards. The concept "up and down" might appear in their geometry, but it would be entirely beyond the reach of their understanding or imagination. Yet a three-dimensional human being would find it natural and simple to bend this two-dimensional world upwards or downwards. This action would, of course, cause phenomena in the two-dimensional world which could not be explained with the laws of a two-dimensional physics. Likewise, if man recognized the necessity of a coordinating phenomenon or a higher order for the explanation of the more profound vectors of life, he might never be able to visualize and sense its true nature.

So far, "animate versus inanimate" has been confronted from a descriptive rather than causalistic or dynamic point of view, but now aspects of cybernetics are introduced into the picture. We find the harmony and the discipline of the action of living organisms unequaled by any kind of inanimated matter. It could be shown that the very complicated, and for man, confusingly complex actions of living matter are controlled by a group of atoms which represent a mere fraction of the total volume of the cell. Even the dislocation of a few of these atoms in a germ cell will cause a dramatic change in large scale hereditary characteristics of the total.

It can be seen that the governing atoms in a cell tend to produce actions which display powerful orderliness and a unique way of maintaining themselves.

Yet, it is a common misconception, even by the well educated layman, that the occurrences of nature, governed by the laws of physics, are the consequence of a well defined and orderly action of atoms. This, however, is only true if a very great number of atoms are observed in the same action. Should the scientist be able to observe a single atom, disregarding its billion companions, he would find complete irregularity in its action. Only the statistical data of innumerable atoms regarded as a unit or interacting system will result, in most of the aspects of "life," in what is called a physical law. If a grain of radium is observed, it can be predicted with certainty that in about eighteen hundred years there will be only a half a grain of radium due to the disintegration of the atoms, but the chance to predict the lifetime of *any single atom within the grain* of radium is less than negligible. It can vary between the next second and millions of years.

On the other hand, in living matter a few specially organized atoms, forming a molecule and existing only in a singular copy, will produce actions which follow seemingly metaphysical laws. These molecules are reproducing themselves but still remain in various respects marvelously tuned-in with each other and their environment; *a truly cybernetic, self-organizing system.*

It seems to be evident that the actions of these governing atoms in highly specialized molecules are guided by laws entirely different from the statistical or probability mechanism of the atoms of the inanimate world, although they may use the same physical tools, which are responsible for shape or form of inanimate matter, such as polarity, bond energies, etc.

The most fundamental laws of physics are based on atomic or molecular disorder. And the law of entropy, the trend of the energy of the Universe, is nothing but molecular disorder itself. It has been shown that in physical laws organization and coordination appear from a disorganized state, whereas, in the laws of life an orderliness of highest order will result in another paragon of orderliness.

Going a step further and regarding the physical phenomena of life and human nature, the possibility of the application of the basic physical laws becomes even more remote. Should man, in his tendency toward materialistic explanation, go so far as to assume that his body is functioning as a purely physical and chemical mechanism, he will have to admit that he is able to direct in certain ways the motions of the atoms of his body. He will foresee the effects and will take full responsibility for them. This will bring the scientist, if he is a true thinker, to the concept of his conscious mind, a mind with the impression of the totality of his experiences and memory. He refers to this unit as "I," the system as "MAN."

It is doubtless that this unit of personality, which evidently cannot be governed by the common physical laws, cannot be subdivided. On the other hand, a person can lose part of his memories and with it part of his personality—and will still survive.

All of this is still the introduction to the aspect of extra-terrestrial intelligence and its influence on our philosophical approach to the cosmos.

Leaving the microcosmos, let us indulge for a moment in the aspects of the macrocosmos.*

There is a new dimension in man's dictionary for concepts: space; and another dimension: time.

Since the dawn of humanity, man has looked up in the sky and called it "heaven." It was considered in many religions the locale of divinity. It was unmeasurable and unapproachable. Now we are storming heaven by pushing our vertical frontier upwards. Man has already put his foot in the door, and it shall not take long before he has developed the tools which can carry him to the stars.

The Universe represents, so man thinks, the unique, exclusive and self-evident feature of existence, and man is attempting to conquer it. But there is, it seems, an inherent limitation in man which *a priori* shatters any such attempt. This is man's limited life span which, in the foreseeable future, will probably not exceed 120 years. On the other hand, in crossing over galactic distances, Nature has set a speed limit which, according to present human knowledge, cannot be overcome without the utter destruction of the system. This limit is the speed of light. This speed limit and the human age limit set a well defined barrier for the human grasp of the universe. It seems almost logically true that this time barrier cannot be overcome.

It is thinkable, of course, that the human age limit of about 120 years, which is determined by the zero turnover rate* of cardiac muscle cells, will be prolonged by some, so far unknown, protein synthesis enhancement in the human body. Also, the speed of light is a fixed universal factor in vacuum only; in other media it can vary considerably, as is demonstrated by the Cerenkov radiation.* Man may utilize this phenomenon for faster than "light" speeds, and in the next centuries or millenia may overcome this barrier. However, no short cuts seem possible in the near future. Yet, as could be demonstrated by meson physics,* the man of this century has already made a breakthrough in this time barrier.

Time dilation in the relativistic domain is a proven fact, and the human mind can compute that by travelling close to the speed of light it would take not more than possibly 40 to 45 years of his biological lifetime to cross the physical universe. That during this relative time-span the material system from where he started has aged millions of years is only of indirect concern to the traveler.

There is still another barrier left, namely, the strangeness of space which, due to the very physical structure of man, will remain alien and hostile. But were the air and the solid land not just as strange, hostile and alien to the creatures of the Cambrian sea? Yet in the millions of years they could adapt themselves to conquer hostile environments. They could do so because of Nature's organization. Are we the insignificant creatures on the lowest level of an evolution in a confinement, in another Cambrian sea? Are we not storming similarly the new dimensions of space and time to which we may adapt ourselves in some hundred millions of years?

Unbelievable? Yes. Unthinkable? No.

So far, an insurmountable barrier has been placed between animate and inanimate matter. In the light of some new engineering sciences, such as cybernetics, bionics, etc., we have to consider the possibility that this chasm between "living" and "non-living" is not as insurmountable as many people think. The first conclusion seems to be that the more intelligent the organism, the more it will be able to close the gap.

If it is assumed that there is intelligent life in extra-terrestrial space, then the thought must be accepted that they may be at a much higher intelligence than ours. Consequently, they may have already arrived at a state where there is no gap between Nature's processes and artifacts generated by these creatures or by the artifacts themselves.

There is nothing bewildering in this thought. Nature builds a man by using certain chemical and physical procedures, utilizing natural resources called metabolites to produce a metazoic aggregate with specific capabilities. Why would it be inconceivable for Nature on another system to utilize entirely different resources, such as a transistor or a diode or capacitor, and build an organism which is capable of all or even more activities than man?

Molectronics, the science of electronic components built from a few molecular aggregates, is already in our reach and a reality. In the same vein, modern parthenogenesis* is in progress to prove how in a primitive inanimate world elementary building blocks of life can originate under the influence of environmental factors and the law of large numbers. Thus, one will be willing to accept the thought that special molecular aggregates, forming a rectifier* or a flip-flop circuit* could, given the benefit of the law of large numbers, assemble themselves into units of highest complexity. Complicated units, such as yeast cells or apples, are quite familiar resources for making a terrestrial man, by feeding them to a self-organizing system and cycling their entropy.* But, if you would obtain the amino acids, glycogen, etc., in bottles and be told that a living man can be built from them with the aid of microscopic chemical assembly lines, the genes, you would be puzzled. How can this concern itself with body functions such as hemodynamics—the flow property of blood—the interaction of actin and myosin in the contraction of a muscle fiber, or the mechanism of the hormone villikinine, which activates the cilia on your small intestine to promote the flow of nutrient from the outside world (which the lumen* of your intestines is considered to be) into your internal environment?

This brings us to the basic principle of systems engineering, namely, that a complex system may show properties which are more or different than the sum total of the capabilities of its parts. Those who know from laboratory experience how very complex systems behave feel that Claud Bernard's* statement that, "It is the subordination of the parts to the whole which knits a complex being into an individual" refers to both living and the so-called inanimate entities. This defeats the monistic thesis that an organism is *simply* a multitude of operational components which work in unison.

Let us now examine other life forms which may be encountered "out there." Let us try to integrate evolutionary and genetic design with invented mechanisms or artifacts which seem just as "natural" as an organism. Without doubt, it is a legitimate conclusion that the integration of a device into an organism for the purpose of increasing its efficiency does not alter its being "alive." It seems also true that the number of such artifacts implanted, for instance, in a man, has practical but not theoretical limits as long as the implant is justified by utility. It is now conceivable that even the *hoi polloi** of an extra-terrestrial super society have a very large number of such devices applied to their bodies to extend their homeostatic* limits and improve their performance. This obviously would not alter their status as living creatures. It is also thinkable, although admittedly in a science fiction fashion, that their upper class can afford equipment which improves their thinking processes. Thus, they could close the gap between man and machine. That is the concept as it exists on Earth in these years, which is, of course, a very anthropocentric approach. However, in the past few years new sciences have developed which project us as Homo Sapiens already entering into this science fiction reality. Such sciences are bionics, cybernetics, systems analysis, automatic control theories, information theories, probability theories, etc.

Before their application is discussed in a Cyborg, meaning "cybernetic organism," or we penetrate into the aims of the society "Artorga," standing for "artificial organisms," one should mention here the trend among thinkers to go beyond the mind-body problem and the integrated man-machine concept, into an interdependence of higher order.

Monism in the sense of Haeckel seems to be inadequate to account for certain phenomena in Nature; dualism is more satisfying to many scientific minds. But as a result of mental extrapolation from the foreseeable futuristic development in the aforementioned new sciences as a point of departure, the philosophy of pluralism seems to emerge.

This approach to the cosmos, as it is known, as supposedly it is known, and as it is known that we don't know it, is a doubt in the absolute validity of basic laws of reality. This in itself is not new, but dozens of philosophers who subscribed to this rationale are not going to be quoted. The Greeks (who else would?) have thought about such things. The Epicureans tried to bridge over the gap, between uncertain events and certain facts with their *clinamen* which is a trend or tendency, or the universal soul or *pneuma* of the Stoics and, even better, Anaxagoras in 500 B.C. with his concept of *Nous,* the intelligence of the Universe.

The novel philosophical approach is that instead of the duality of body and soul there could be a multitude of higher order of interdependent essentials which govern reality and "metaphysical" entities.

The concept of cybernetic pluralism obtains good impetus from certain aspects of atomic physics. Here, Sir James Jeans* helps with his remark that, "The stream of knowledge is heading towards a non-material reality; the universe begins to look more like a great thought than like a great machine."

The study of the microcosmos and through it the macro-cosmos, reveals a pyramid of vectors, a matrix, a pluralism, if you please, which are the essentials in the static and dynamic maintenance of the cosmos. It is even questionable whether there exists a steady state of matter if viewed from its microcosmos. The

factors which establish matter, including anti-matter,* are obviously at a lower part of the pyramid of vectors, and contain but do
not reveal in a simple fashion the common denominator.

The philosophy of pluralism does not seek really the ultimate
common denominator, but emphasizes that, in contrast to the
matter-soul duality in the Christian sense, there are a number of
essentially different parameters which manifest themselves in the
forming of our perceivable universe.

There is, for instance, the riddle of the electron, the nature of
which completely defies human apperception. And virtual mesons
or the neutrino are no less problematic. Yet there is, no doubt, the
same fundamental mechanism operating in the material reality of
all inanimate and animate matter.

Not excluding the theoretical possibility of new types of
energy forms, such as psychokinetics,* one would assume that
such factors as the dichotomy of energy and matter, the relative
value of time and some other aspects of modern physics should be
explored and then related to phenomena of the "living" matter.

It may turn out that the search for a unified concept,
including a unified field theory, is only an inherent pattern of
human behavior which relentlessly pursues a universal oneness
from which it can derive all and everything. *Nature does not have
to be built like that.* Why could there not be a pluralism of
incongruent factors which, literally, make up the universe? From
the point of view of cosmogenesis such a concept does not have
less logic than Gamov's* primordial explosion or the continuous
creation theory.

The reader may wonder what the purpose was in the
explanation of "information" via the term "life" in such an
expansion. The writer feels that it illuminates not only the huge
information content of the four-letter code "life," but it shows
also the dynamism of associated mental processes when the human
brain receives the coded signal "life," which initiate a line of
complex thoughts.

Instead of indulging further in such very broad aspects of the
problem, it seems more fruitful to discuss briefly the systems
analysis of organized matter.

The term "systems analysis" has to be taken here in its
broadest sense.

THE SYSTEMS APPROACH

There is no self respecting biology teacher today who would not teach to his freshman biology class the marvels of homeostasis and the intricacies of feedback.*

There is no doubt in most scientists' minds, that, according to our present knowledge, self-organization, of which homeostasis and feedback are the backbone, is responsible for evolution on earth; and it seems that self-organization plays an enormous role in the inanimate world, too. By definition, living, self-organizing systems have negative entropy, and one of the modern definitions of life rests on this phenomenon. It states that if a system is capable of utilizing disorganized molecules, and if it assembles them dynamically into a system of higher organization, thus displaying negative entropy, then it is alive.

A growing crystal has, of course, negative entropy; we don't know exactly how that form aids it to maintain an equilibrium and increases its survival value against the variable stresses of its environment.

Furthermore, there are innumerable electronic circuitry designs which maintain a certain state; and if they are forced by external factors into a different state, they will return every time and without external influence, automatically, to their original homeostatic state.

As the reader can see, the term "automatic" enters into our discussion at this point. This term is one of the most misused and misunderstood expressions in semantics and communication. But before some of the aspects of *automation* are discussed, it should be mentioned that the laws of homeostasis seem to be all-embracing; for example, if one could give all environmental factors and any of their changes in the past few millions of years on Mars, and if one would, for the sake of simplicity, exclude the crucial factors of probability and time, then it could be determined with some certainty whether the men on Mars are small, green and with two tentacles on their heads.

Now back to automation. The term itself is dimensionless and, unless it is quantified, it stays meaningless. It is obvious that when you step on the gas pedal, your car will automatically increase its speed. By the way, don't forget that the carburetor is a typical self-organizing system which keeps the level of fuel dynamically constant in a container, regardless of the rate of consumption.

An inertial guidance platform* which keeps a missile on a course is obviously a more complex automat. And if we regard Elmer* or Elsie* we have arrived to the *machina speculatrix** and the *machina docilis.** The family of these cybernetic machines or mechanical organisms has already another member, the *machina judicatrix.** The latter is quite talented as far as moron machines go. It can choose between a hot and noisy room and a cold and quiet room. It does exhibit feelings because as long as its batteries are charged to 8 volts it emits a continuous purring sound. However, if the voltage is dropped below 3 volts, it runs around and growls. Its sister, Elsie the turtle, is smarter. If you command her to perform, for instance, to go through a maze, her batteries may run down. But at a safe time when this danger exists, Elsie will retreat, plug herself into a wall socket and recharge her batteries. Well-fed, she goes back to the maze, but due to her memory she will bypass all dead-end roads which she experienced before. This is amazing, but to me it is even more amazing that sometimes she will make a mistake and try a blind alley which she should have *known* leads to nowhere.

The next step was to reproduce conditioned reflexes in the Pavlovian* sense. If this can be accomplished, then the door is open to educational processes in machines.

This machine, called CORA for Conditioned-Reflex-Analog, was born in a parthenogenetic manner from the parts of Elsie.

When Cora was young, she had a light-sensing organ and an audio organ, an ear, if you wish. This microphone was functional and registered sound, but it initiated no response because she was not yet trained. As Grey Walter* developed a theory of conditioned reflexes, he realized that the neural network responsible for it could be translated into electronic circuitry, and he built it into Cora. If light was applied to Cora which activated a circuit and promised "food" (just as a dog gets a morsel for a performance) and at the same time a sound was uttered which could be perceived by the mechanism, after a number of repetitions, Cora associated the sound with the appearance of the light. From then on it responded to the sound even if there was no light signal.

This and numerous other amazing and unbelievable examples show very clearly that cybernetics can and will demonstrate that our concept of the artifact "machine" was a false one and for the sake of communication our vocabulary should be refined and reserve that term for a dynamo, a crane or a locomotive.

A more recent performance of Cora was the association of noise and bumping. Anytime Cora bumped into an obstacle, her master blew a whistle. After certain training Cora moved around the obstacle if her master signaled with the sound. It is not too difficult to imagine replacing sound with a visual sensation, and then a dog or a cat would not perform any differently in this respect. As a matter of fact, this concept has been utilized already to replace the limited speed of visual perception, the decision forming and the psychomotor function of man. In high performance supersonic low-flying aircraft, collision avoidance could not be left with the pilot. At 1000 miles per hour speed, flying 50 to 80 feet altitude over the terrain, an obstacle may appear at a 1000-foot distance, and within a half-second a pilot would have already crashed into it. Obviously, the human machinery cannot cope with this condition, but an electronic organism will perceive the signal, recognize it as an obstacle, decide the necessity of a maneuver and actuate the attitude and control mechanism in not more than one one hundredth of a second.

MENTALITY

Recently, a young computer programmer at RCA fed, at random, a number of words into the computer with the program that the words should be sequenced in four lines, eight or ten words per line. To his great astonishment he found among the many nonsense groups of words also very good poetry.

Then there is the family of Perceptrons. These were at first quite normal computers, but they became more and more sophisticated. Now the Perceptron C can compose music and invent geometrical laws. In other words, it became a machine which possesses a truly human quality, namely, intuition.

And just what is intuition or invention in the cybernetic sense? The requisites for it are: 1) information, that is data of observations and deductions; 2) facility of learning; 3) inventiveness; and, maybe, 4) luck, which is, in a more scientific lingo, "skewed randomness," whatever that means. The definition of inventiveness can be the "subconscious assembly of memorized data with a chance match of random information to a desired or requested pattern in both the positive or the negative sense."

Before the last but not least aspect of our basic topic, the probability of extra-terrestrial life, let us briefly mention the cybernetic task which would make it possible for the astronaut to get out of a spaceship on Jupiter, walk quickly fifty feet and pick up a pebble from the ground. This task does not seem very formidable; the first systems analysis showed that one has to consider in approximation only two environmental parameters, namely, gravity and the Jovian atmosphere. The Jovian atmosphere, as we think we know it, consists of hydrogen, methane, ammonia under high pressure, and lots of highly corrosive free radicals.* The gravity is about 2.6 times that of the Earth on the Jovian surface, provided there is a surface in the terrestrial sense. It could be that the immense atmospheric gases have, under the influence of the high gravity, a density gradient which at a point may have the consistency of a wet marshland on Earth. But for simplicity's sake it can be decided that the face of Jupiter is a nice solid rock.

A man on Jupiter and his armored space suit, which must withstand the high pressure and the corrosion and which contains instruments and a power plant, could weigh maybe 3500 pounds. To work against the inertia and the weight of such a body the human capability is utterly inadequate.

The solution to the problem is that the action potential* of the muscles may be harnessed, fed through a computer into a relay system which actuates sturdy electric motors, which, in turn, can move the arm or leg of the suit. If one decides to bend an arm in a certain way, one commands the *biceps brachii** to contract and the arm will snap. At the same instance an electric current will be fed into a relay which will actuate a motor strong enough to do the same with the 500-pound space suit arm. If one wants to do the motion slowly, he simply actuates simultaneously the *biceps* and the *triceps*, (the latter muscle moves the arm in the opposite direction). Very simple.

Now let us look into the extension of these bionic devices into the realm of mental processes.

One of the big mistakes of the pre-cybernetics scientists in their attempts to comprehend the true working scheme of the brain was that it was left in the hands of classical neurophysiologists. Most of them don't know enough mathematics and circuit theories, and not even a handful understand Shannon's theorems* and the law of requisite variety.* Some people also believe that a good, thinking brain can predict the future, at least to some degree; but the truth is that working in the future means really to manipulate the past. However, only if the past is in a steady state, or if the time function of the past has monotonously changing dependent variables, can the brain arrive at certain conclusions concerning the future. The brain is a goal-seeking device with good data processing capabilities. The crucial point is the efficiency by which the goal is recognized. If the goal is known and the starting point, then the necessary mental work for problem solving will drop by its square root. For example, we express neural functions of the brain with a million operations; then, if the goal is known, it requires only a thousand operations. That means that the finding of the goal has an efficiency of one-tenth of one percent. Here lies the future of cybernetics—designing systems with much higher *rendement.** But first, we must know more about the laws of the trial and error processes of biological systems and the properties of manifold equilibria, namely systems which exist in many stable equilibria.

So far, we have skimmed over various aspects of how man is storming the Universe. He does it not only in his attempt of mastering distance, time and matter, but also in his effort to improve mankind; improve it not in the evolutionary sense by slowly eliminating the least fit, but by artificially extending the capabilities of his frail body. On this road he not only implants components to achieve better efficiency of the system, MAN, but also tries to design machines to which he is willing to hand over all characteristics which, so far, have been considered uniquely human. This includes self-reproducing machines which assemble themselves from simple components in their environment or, as the Russian mathematician Kremjansky figures it, will go and seek out the necessary components or raw materials. In a further technological and very futuristic step, man probably will be able to improve greatly these characteristics; and he hopes that he can control this super-human machine.

So far, so good, but recently man has been trying to increase his bodily capabilities along lines for which Nature needed millions of years. It is a very feeble attempt but so was bionics just ten years ago. Micrurgy* and the manipulation of genes could, theoretically, bring about marvels so fantastic that, in comparison, the wildest guesses of the most uninhibited science fiction writer would look like the caveman's club compared to a nuclear intercontinental missile.

In artificial eugenics man has arrived at a point where he starts tampering with humanity. One wonders whether this is permissible; whether the *licentia scienciae** has no restrictions. Is the aim of science not the increase of knowledge and the servitude for human happiness? Or, is this an obsolete terrestrial viewpoint? Is a galactic morality not infinitely far ahead of us? This opens the door for our final deliberation.

What are the chances to find life forms in space which are comparable with man even in the most remote sense?

According to statistics, the probability of an event is inversely proportional to the size of the causal field.* This statement alone, if true, would render the chance of the aforementioned exobiology* negligible. I think it best to quote a few scientists of stature whose word deserves attention but not necessarily credence.

Shapely, in his book *Of Stars and Men,* estimates that life of some sort exists on more than 100 million planets in the universe. He considers it "reasonable" to assume that on many planets evolutionary forces brought about higher life-forms, some of which have gone already much further than the present state of humanity.

A serious enterprise, called "Project Ozma" after the queen of the Land of Oz, "a place very far away, difficult to reach and populated by exotic beings," deals with the assumption that advanced societies did evolve and are signaling with some sort of radio waves. Now they are waiting patiently for our answer. Of course, the transmission is weak and the signal-to-noise ratio is very unfavorable. This is due to the background radiation from the sun and the galaxy. The region with relatively little noise is near the 10^{10} cycles per second wavelength band. And close to this frequency, at 14×10^{10} cps wavelength, is a standard which must be known to every electronically educated observer all over the universe—the radio emission line of neutral hydrogen.

In the Spring of 1960 an attempt was made to detect such signals. The 85-foot radio telescope at Green Bank, West Virginia, was trained on Tau Ceti and Epsilon Eridam, which are about 10 light years away. There was no message, at least none which we could receive with this instrument. These were only two stars in many billions; but Gadomski* describes 16 solartype stars, the planets of which could carry life within 17 light years of radius from the sun.

Bracewell, in his article, "Communications from Superior Galactic Communities," which appeared in *Nature,* 1960, suggests that the nearest community is over 100 light years away. But instead of signals these communities probably have sent probes into the star systems which show the prerequisites for higher life forms. These devices would go into orbit around the target objects, send as well as receive messages and try to make contact with the intelligentsia. (Much luck to the "Flying Saucer" watchers!)

A discussion in two issues of *Nature,* in 1960, warrants attention. Dyson, from nowhere other than the Institute of Advanced Studies in Princeton, proposed the hypothesis that a technologically far-advanced race may have created from the matter of their home planet a shell around their sun to most effectively use the radiation from their source of energy. Therefore, this would be dark from the outside but would emit excess infrared radiation in the 10 micron range. He suggests that we should look for such objects in this galaxy.

In November, 1961, a scientific meeting was held in Green Bank, West Virginia, with an attendance of leading scientists. *The New York Times* reported that the papers read in the meeting were greatly controversial. Some predicted the impossibility of interstellar travel; others described the actual techniques to be used in contacting civilizations on other planets. Again others described the methods to detect life on other planets of our solar system. Such devices are already on the drawing boards or in form of prototypes at the National Aeronautics and Space Administration.

On the other hand, Hibbs, in his article entitled "Life on Other Worlds," which appeared in the January 1, 1961 issue of the *Los Angeles Times,* is much more pessimistic and fears that if we pursue our reckless venture of contacting alien societies in space we might find ourselves in an embarrassing situation because, rated by our intelligence, our relative position of a domestic animal is undoubtedly the very best we could expect. He concludes that it would be imprudent to try to signal other societies.

It seems that only a minority is doubting that man will ever encounter life of higher intelligence in space. Maybe these gentlemen are either astronomers or biologists but are not initiated in the exclusive club of astrobiology.

There are three factors in favor of the minority: 1) Although there are about 10^{23} stars in the universe, how many have planets? From these how many are in the thermal region of the bio-sphere? Of these how many have atmosphere? Of these how many atmospheres are biologically compatible? From these how many have water? From these, how many have all other environmental factors which are the *conditio sine qua non** for life? These questions shave off a great number of decimals from the 10^{23}. Is anything left? Who knows? 2) Intelligence is definitely related to our brain structure and the interrelation of its neurons. Now, we have about 10^{11} neurons in the brain, which had to evolve in just the right way to bring about the pattern which could organize into an intelligent man. Furthermore, one cannot see any forcing function in the development of the brain which would require a gradient pattern from the more primitive or just different neural configuration into the network of Homo Sapiens. The thus far accepted Darwinian theory of evolution through successful mutants could have taken thousands of favorable pathways, none of which had to lead to or culminate in the brain of Man. What chance is there for redundancy, even assuming millions of planets with potential supporting conditions of life? 3) Finally, assuming that the low figure of probability is still significant in the above two factors, then the time-space element will help the argument in the realistic sense. If there can exist creatures with at least human intelligence, then they may have existed a billion years ago or will come about a billion years hence. And if they exist now but are a billion light years away, what are the odds to ever find them? Unless—but that would weaken the argument and carry us into science fiction.

So far, the above discussion has had little direct bearing on the development of a philosophical thesis which would look at the Universe from a new angle. Yet the unifying of the pluralism of living and non-living matter must necessarily begin with the analysis of the component to be followed by the search for a common denominator. This is as far as we wish to carry the discussion at this time.

It seems the fact has been established that the manifestations of life, in the common sense of semantics, do not constitute a uniqueness, a *conditio sine qua non,* but an assembly of symptoms, many of which can be not just simulated by so-called inanimate matter, but truly reproduced. As human knowledge progresses, these artifacts will become more and more perfect in initiating and surpassing organismic characteristics, and it seems highly probable that the time will come, and maybe sooner than we anticipate, where those definitions which today define organic life will have to be changed radically. The other avenue which man pursues in molecular biology, namely, artificial parthenogenesis, may yield results which will also add to the degradation of the concept of the uniqueness of life.

Furthermore, molectronics has already demonstrated, so far in a primitive way, that small molecular aggregates can be obtained which are the significant and essential parts of those artifacts which, in turn, are showing interchangeable characteristics with systems called "intelligent life."

Regarding these sub-sciences, we can find already signs of the common denominator. The proper assembly of select molecular units in a highly specific environment can and will bring about an agglomeration of certain entities, which will show the unique behavior which generally is termed "living."

This line of reasoning opens the door for speculation concerning the possibility of other types of molecular aggregates performing systems behavior, under again highly specific environmental conditions which would be called organismic. In this, the theoretical possibility for the existence of extra-terrestrial organisms is established. How high the probability of such occurrence is in the physical universe, as we know it today, is, of course, not even approximated.

The only further suggestion to be added to this is that the uniqueness of human life, with the emotional content called by Christians, "soul," is but an intuitive, restrictive expression of a more universal trend of organization which is inherent in the plurality of physical entities.

Such a trend of negative entropy may well be the greatest asset of the universe as viewed from a cosmocentric point, because it could constitute the counter balance in the dynamic equilibrium of matter where "life" is an interesting and, for us, vitally important manifestation of a purpose.

Should it turn out, however, that "intelligent life" in the human sense is restricted to Terra, and assemblies with at least human capabilities are not found elsewhere, then our approach to the philosophy of existence will have to be revised. At any rate, we can expect that in the next centuries our outlook on life will be substantially modified. The vectors which will bring about such change will come from two directions, molecular biology and physics. Whether more information on the neutrino would become a significant factor remains to be seen.

In conclusion, it seems that: 1) There are no fundamental differences between living creatures, obtained without human influence, and certain "artifacts," constructed with the aid of man. Those "exclusively" human characteristics as virtue and the appreciation of beauty may some day be incorporated into artifacts by the science of robotics,* which has already obtained academic status. 2) Life seems to be a systems phenomenon, the components of which must be looked for at the molecular level. Marvelous organs and differentiated cells are homeostatic subsystems with, so far, incomprehensible programming. 3) The energetics of the material world are quite complex, and the subdivision into the physical and biological forces is an intolerable oversimplification. It seems rather mandatory that a number of force vectors, quite different in characteristics, constitute the condition under which all matter "exists" in a transcendental sense. These condition parameters, although incongruent, are not incompatible. This is logical because otherwise they could not be part of the whole. If psychokinesis is found and becomes a science, it will probably not contradict the second law of thermodynamics. 4) Plurality, by definition, does not deal with the concept of a primordial organizer, although such a topic may fit well into this philosophy. It can be expected that as millenia of human progress pass and if *Homo Sapiens* still exists or is even modified into *Homo Coelorum,** the concept of God will become more rational than the servitude beliefs of the man in the dark middle ages.

What is new, one may ask, in this approach to understand and, if possible, visualize the physical reality of life and the fundamental organization of matter in the cosmic pattern?

Before answering this question, it should be mentioned that the lack of visualization would be but a small obstacle, because the rejection of concepts by the human mind or the lack of perception of physical or metaphysical facts may just show the limits of the human brain in its present state. There is no logic which would indicate that Nature cannot be built in a way that certain of its configurations defy the human mind; although, it seems that the brain is able to adapt itself and to become capable of utilizing inconceivable concepts. For instance, it is probable that Kant or Déscartes would have been unable to comprehend or accept the "principle of uncertainty"* or the possibility of virtual mesons,* even if certain mathematical or experimental facts would have been accessible to them. Today we have little difficulty to live with virtual mesons or the intricacies of neutrino physics, none of which can be "visualized."

There are a number of good books and articles dealing with the most recent concept of matter *per se,* the cosmos as a system, or molecular biology as the tool for the approximation of primordial parthenogenesis. Some of these are listed in the bibliography. Some of these writings deal also with the logic of the spiritual rather than the materialistic approach to these problems. All of these philosophical-technical attempts are dealing primarily with one or the other aspects of biocosmology.

The shortcoming of this is that they consider only a discrete number of specific existentialistic parameters, which are, no doubt, all important from their special point of view. However, to borrow a figurative example from acoustics, they are only like the harmonics or the interaction of complex frequencies and wave-shaped patterns.

The novel approach in this present attempt is that one is looking for some sort of Fourier analysis* (to follow the figurative example) with which one can detect the fundamentals and the interference nodes which should give insight into a unified picture of the living and the inanimate world. The time has come when we should be bold enough and attempt to approach and possibly comprehend the total system of the cosmos. Hereby we are paying special attention to the nature and significance of living matter and the concept of intelligence and their place in the cosmic matrix.

So far, valiant approaches have been made by our best minds but, depending on their training and background, only parts of the problem syndrome have been illuminated. In general, a cosmologist is not also a cybernetician, or a molecular biologist does not have the depth of knowledge in astronomy. Unfortunately, this truly interdisciplinary problem cannot be solved by attacking *pars pro toto*.

3.

THE LIMITS OF INFORMATION

If one is using the term "limit," it means a gradient of some static parameter or dynamic event. As a figure of speech, one talks about an upper and a lower extreme which constitutes the limits.

Dealing with the limits of information, one looks, on one hand, for the smallest unit below which the term information, which refers to the *transmission of intelligence,* has no meaning. On the other hand, the upper limits of information need a more precise definition, because one may refer to the upper limit of information storage, the upper limit of information flux in a given medium or, in more general terms, the approximation of an upper limit or sum total of all information which can be made available to man for decision purposes.

This brief chapter will deal with this latter aspect. But first, a few words should be said about the lowest limit of information, although that is better known and explored than the upper limit.

To define the lower limit, or unit of information, would be a too ambitious undertaking for this brief presentation, because it would entail the discussion of information theories, also called communication theories. It is much more proper to refer to the books which deal exhaustively with this question, such as

Shannon's pioneer, 1949 study *The Mathematical Theory of Communication.*

It should suffice to state here that the basic unit of information is one "bit." This term is the abbreviation of "binary digit" and refers to a simple probability or uncertainty. The unit "bit" determines the choice between two equal in value but oppositely directed states of an unbiased source. For example, the appearance of heads or tails of a good coin, the presence or absence of a symbol, a lamp to be lit or not lit, etc.

The measure of information by Shannon is expressed in entropy, a term which is well known to all who have had dealings with thermodynamics. In reference to information, the term "entropy of a message" provides the measure and the number of bits which are necessary to encode the message, or, in other words, necessary to make it intelligible.

This writer feels the urge to go into greater depth by describing with much more detail these basic aspects of the information theories. But he is confronted with a decision: either he wants to see this chapter published or he does not want to see this chapter published. This decision is related to one bit of information. If he chooses the first alternative, then he cannot describe in detail the basic aspects of the information theories, because the publisher does not provide the space for it. If he does not want to see this chapter published, he can describe the information theories in great detail. But to keep it in his drawer without being able to transmit his message defies the purpose of a message. Therefore, he decided to see this chapter published. (However, with this sentence he has cheated his publisher, because he demonstrated a very important aspect of the information theories, namely, the channel capacity, or band-width.* Hopefully, the reader is by now well-motivated to get a book on the information theories and read about that which is omitted here.)

Now the time (and space) has come to look into the upper limits of information. Terms such as data processing, data handling, information transmission, etc., are today part of the vocabulary of newspapers, magazines and popular literature. Just a few years ago, only highly technical reports, advanced engineering courses and the like used these expressions in connection with abstract aspects of information and communication theories, and with more practical aspects of astronautics—communication in space and in missilry in general.

Information theories were considered as a rather esoteric science, accessible only to a very few specialists and not understandable for even the technically trained engineers and scientists. This reminds us of the decades after the publication of the special theory of relativity in 1905. One assumed that only Einstein and a very few like him could make this theory meaningful; yet today it is a high school topic.

Basically, information theories are very simple, as are other basic laws in Nature. However, it is doubtful that information theory is nothing other than a form of counting, as has been suggested. This seems to be an oversimplification to a degree where the meaning of the term does not match the meaning of the principle which it is supposed to describe.

One may exemplify information theories by stating that if there is an unmanned space probe flying which can, upon radio command, perform ten different and independent functions, then its capabilities could not be controlled by only five simple signals.

There are, of course, other problems involved in transmitting intelligence from one point to another. For instance, one limitation is the interference which may come from the environment or from the transmitting device, which includes man. The interference, called noise, is very cumbersome and sometimes greatly reduces the intelligibility of the information. Shannon and Wiener have shown, however, how one can more or less extract the intelligent signal from a noisy transmission.

Another paramount limitation of information transmission is the fundamental slowness of any action requiring a finite, irreducible amount of time and the fundamental "graininess" of all matter, which indicates that volume and mass are a step-function, rather than a gradient. These facts set a well-defined limit to the flux of information, which is the flow of a number of bits per second.

Bremerman* could show that due to certain quantum restrictions* of matter, regardless of the perfection of the receiving station and the efficiency of the transmitter, the maximum-information that anybody or anything could handle is 10^{47} bits per gram per second.

At first this seems to be a very satisfactory quantity, especially if one takes tons of computers and years of transmitting time into consideration. But if one regards a ton of even the most efficient equipment, which is equal to 10^6 grams, this raises the figure 10^{47} only to 10^{53}. Considering now a whole century for transmitting information, one deals with 10^{12} seconds, which in turn, raises the original 10^{47} only to 10^{65}. As one can see, the increase of mass in the information handling equipment or the stretching of time to many generations does not greatly alter the value of the exponential. No matter how much future solid state devices will be perfected, or how large or complex the computers are which will be built, the number of bits of information handling capability would be altered only by a very few units.

But as soon as one looks into a brain or brain-like structure, and looks especially at the information flux inherent in such structures, one realizes the realm of truly large numbers, one could almost say astronomical numbers—but in a different sense than this expression is generally used, because "astronomical numbers" are not frightfully large. For instance, a microsecond, which is one one-millionth of a second, is a very short time; but if the microseconds since the hardening of the earth's crust were totalled, they would amount to only 10^{23} microseconds. The total number of atoms in the physical universe is somewhere near 10^{73}. To obtain an even larger "astronomical figure," one can take an average atomic event which lasts about 10^{-10} seconds and total the number of seconds with the number of all atoms in the universe, as we know it, back to the time when the earth started to solidify; we arrive at the figure of about 10^{100}. It is, of course, possible to imagine or compute much larger numbers, but they would not be representing physical reality. This was Bremerman's original argument too.

After this brief survey the reader will appreciate more the large numbers which occur if one analyzes information processes. The example given by Ross Ashby* is a square with 20 x 20 lamps. Each of these 400 lamps can be on or off and each represents one bit of information. The total amount of information represented by all combinations of the on and off positions of the 400 lamps is 2^{400} which is 10^{120} in approximation.

If one is confronted with an information display of this relatively primitive type and is given the task to look for a certain pattern of the lit lamps, his brain is exposed to and is searching a total information of 10^{120} bits, which at first, seems quite incredible. Although one can compute such numbers easily, the human brain completely lacks the ability to get the feel or, as one may put it, the emotional content of the dimension of such a figure.

To exemplify this point, one should consider the figure 10^{80}. It is unlikely that anyone would realize, without being alerted to the fact, that he could not place the units of this number, one unit per atom, on all the atoms in the physical universe, because there are just not enough atoms available.

Another example would be the psychophysical model of the frog's eye, which not only has been designed theoretically, but also has been developed as a working model, or rather a cybernetic or bionic analog. In the same way as in the model of 20 x 20 lamps, it should be assumed that every neuron in the retina of the frog's eye can be excited or not excited. These effectors* will, in combination, convey information to the brain of the frog. Assuming that there are a million such effectors in the eye of the frog, the frog's brain is confronted with $10^{300\,000}$ stimuli.

It is significant that cybernetic research has revealed that the retina in the human eye performs partial data processing of visual information, thus reducing the flux which reaches the brain. In spite of that, the amount of information known to reach the brain is in strong contrast to Bremerman's limit of information, which states that a man can receive, during his lifetime, not more than about 10^{60} bits of information. It can be inferred that the information theories set certain limits for the transmission and reception of information.

No matter how much information man is capable of receiving, even if that number were multiplied by the number of seconds in the lifetime of a man, it would seem very restrictive compared to the combinatorial numbers mentioned above. If one deals with information, it is inescapably necessary to correlate messages with intelligent brains or brain-like machines. It then becomes natural to explore the mechanism by which a brain is utilizing information. It has been found that in processing information, a brain or any brain-like structure will spend a large part of the available time and energy in searching. This is an inherent pattern not only in highly sophisticated, self-sufficient, decision-making brain analogs, but also in more primitive machines, such as chess-playing machines, pattern recognition machines, theorem-proving machines, etc.

One finds that by the searching process, or what amounts to the same thing—by a combinatory matrix of trial and error—the first few steps are quite manageable. However, the number of possible and probable events soon goes into such high figures that it becomes quite unmanageable and the process must be stopped. To use one of Ross Ashby's† examples, it is quite simple to play a game of unbeatable, perfect chess. All that one has to do is to list all developments of possible games and eliminate those which end in check mate, then play any of the remaining developments. But if one tries to attach figures to this task, Bremerman's "upper limit," namely 10^{60} bits of information, renders the human brain quite insignificant, because the figure for a perfect game of chess is in approximation between 10^{120} and $10^{3,000}$ bits. Minsky* has concluded that if one tries to develop a brain or brain-like structure, then the device must have a search capability and must somehow overcome the barrier of very large numbers.

One way to cope with the very large numbers is to restrict the requirement to practical levels. For instance, if one does not want the machine to play the perfect chess game every time, but is satisfied with the machine to win in the majority of cases, then the unmanageably large numbers will be significantly reduced. Further reduction is achieved if the program which has to be computed is specifically goal-directed, that is, to use the above example, if one requests the machine to win a specific game. This would diminish the number by its square root, and instead of a million trials and errors, the computer would have to process only 1,000 bits of information.

Another example mentioned by Ross Ashby† is to use a branched arterial system in which each branch has three consecutive branches with a total of 12 pre-determined branching points.

† Ashby, Ross. Personal communication.

Then the total searching steps are only 3^{12}, which is about a half of one million. If one works with a known goal and searches backwards from the goal, the number of contact points needed to reach the beginning of the family of branches is 3^6 or about 750. The efficiency of this reverse goal-directed search becomes greater as the total number increases. Of course, the proper approach to the problem is not always easy and in some cases it becomes senseless to pursue a reverse search, because it necessitates having the solution of the problem before one can feed the information into a computer. The computer then may only provide the reassurance that the manual solution of the problem is, or is not, correct. Someone has put the two search processes in a very illustrative comparison by saying that the difference in these two methods is like searching a haystack for a needle or shaking a haystack until the needle falls out.

The significance of Bremerman's limit is quite obvious, and it will have an ever-increasing impact on our age of automation. Sophisticated computer designers and large systems analysts especially will have to keep Bremerman's limit in mind, for if all of the 10^{11} neurons in a brain-like device were connected with each other, they would reach far beyond Bremerman's limit in possible information flux, and one would find that the device could not operate or, rather, technically it cannot be designed.

It is important to recognize that the systems approach to components and combinatorial figures has an upper limit beyond which reality does not exist. The existence of such a limit, which at present seems to have an absolute value, will hit hard at philosophers. The fact that a brain weighing 1000 grams cannot process more information than 10^{50} bits per second is a restriction which physiologists and psychologists will find difficult to accept theoretically, although by experience they know how much smaller the brain's capacity is. Computer designers, especially for space or galactic communications, should bear this limit in mind; although it seems that other limiting factors of information theories—such as band-width, available power, transparency of the medium, etc.—will restrict the designers, in most of the cases, before Bremerman's limit will catch up with them.

It should be noted that Bremerman's limit is not compatible with General Systems concepts. In the past couple of decades the systems theories developed from the analysis of the individual events into complex interconnected systems. As this science became more sophisticated, the complexity of the networks increased rapidly. The development of intricate feedback and complex computer processes invited the exploration of the behavior of more and more network interactions. If one extrapolates to large systems, such as interconnecting every nerve in a brain with all other nerves of the same brain, or if one interconnected every logic element in a very large computer with all other elements, or if every person in the United States talked simultaneously to every other person in the United States, one could reach unmanageable combinatorial numbers.

This indicates that new factors have to be taken into careful consideration in the General Systems theories. The time is approaching when the validity of the systems theories will be questioned due to inaccuracies between theory and facts. A refinement of the presently accepted laws of systems is mandatory, as the alteration of views regarding some aspects of classical physics was mandatory when the theory of relativity was developed.

Bremerman's limit as well as other principles of the information theories were then and still are under crossfire. One interesting potshot was when someone challenged the energy dependence of information transmission with the following example: Husband and wife agree that if he comes home for dinner, he will call at 6 o'clock; if he does not call, he will not come. At 6 o'clock the phone did not ring. Thus, without any energy expenditure or any physical disturbance an intelligent message was transmitted from one human to another's brain. This can be further complicated if the wife hears over the radio that shortly before 6 o'clock, due to an explosion, all phones in the city were out of commission; thus, the chance exists that the message was incorrect because he might have tried to call at 6 o'clock. This and other similar examples, like mathematical puzzles, have more or less transparent solutions without providing proof against the information theories.

One last aspect of the limits of information, which has a more practical than theoretical value, is the special capability of the human mind. In playing chess or football, or in military strategy, there is an element which one calls intuition. In intuition, instead of scanning all possible combinations, one relies on what is called "hunch." In many cases this process reduces enormously the time and work required for the solution of the problem. Thus the human brain does use a technique, the mechanism of which is unknown, to reduce combinatorial numbers to manageable dimensions.

Again the limits of information, which can be used for the transmission of intelligence, are brought to the foreground. Obviously much thinking and research are warranted in this field, because the importance of knowledge cannot be underestimated in an epoch when the technology of information handling is skyrocketing.

4.
PRAGMATOSCOPE

A Cybernetic Information Display

It is still the impression of many persons that cybernetics is a philosophical-theoretical faculty, with little or no practical application. Therefore, to prove the invalidity of this point, in the following a few examples will be discussed where the cybernetic approach, namely, *the study of the flow of information, with the subsequent control functions,* provides a solution. The examples are concerned with complex visual information displays.

As in the case of so many scientific developments, the original research was suggested by military need. Regardless of its military utility, the research and development effort will encompass civilian aspects as well. This latter aspect may come simultaneously with the military application, or the attention to it could come later.

In the case of the Pragmatoscope, the possibility for civilian use was recognized, yet by financial necessity the military aspect was developed. For such reasons the Pragmatoscope was designed for military purposes and will be treated here from this angle. It is hoped, however, that the ingenuity of the reader will find many civilian applications.

The development of a new offensive weapons system always triggers research for a corresponding counterweapon. The advent of airborne vehicles for military purposes was no exception. Counterweapons were developed, but the development of adequate sensing sub-systems fell far behind. The invention of radar seemed to be the answer. It was not long, however, before the answer itself was found to contain a problem, namely, how was this radar information to be displayed adequately for decision making and action selection?

Man soon came up with a solution, the Plan Position Indicator or PPI scope. World War II and the Korean Police Action are replete with examples testifying to the adequacy of the radar sensing sub-systems as the terminal display within the limits of aircraft location tasks. Supersonic airplanes, the development of missiles, and the Electronic Counter Measures soon put the PPI scope and all its ramifications through extremely severe tests. To date, researchers and industry have been forced to concentrate their efforts on solutions for refinements of the operational use of various types of cathode ray tube information displays.

The work to be done involves the perfections of but a small part of a large system. Granted, the desired display is a system in itself, and a very complicated one; however, its proper design will be achieved only after a rigorous analysis of the parent system to which it belongs. One is reminded of the oft-quoted saying of von Bertalanffy:* "You cannot be thinking as one interested in General Systems theory without an ecological frame of reference." This means that one man's system is another man's sub-system. It is so in mathematics, physics, biology and any other discipline.

Air defense of a given locale with limited defensive capability is the overall picture into which the proposed display must fit. The display portion of this environment is that part of the parent system which is assigned the task of easing the decision maker's load in carrying out the functions known as threat evaluation and action selection. The Pentomic and Pentana strategy concepts,* which were developed to meet the dynamic requirements of nuclear warfare, need an information display which regards the total battleground; and this may be a total continent instead of small units of friend and foe.

This problem seems a good opportunity to apply the systems approach. The systems approach seems to be the best method of attack for the design of a dynamic information display for the required purpose. A number of displays exists for the commander of various weapon complexes, but in a form which is closely related to the requirements of the weapon system of a by-gone era. They do very little to relieve the user of the immense decision-making problems facing him, with very little time at his command, which aggravates the situation.

The weapon commander is being given more and more data to help him evaluate threat and select an action which is optimum in meeting that threat. However, the complexity of battle situations in the tactical missile age often leaves him insufficient time for proper evaluation and action. The next generation of displays must relieve the commander of the mental strain created by a data overload preceding vital decisions. These are brought about either by small threats which in and of themselves are of little import but when taken together form a major threat, or by a large number of simultaneous catastrophic threats with the possible consequences carried by megaton nuclear warheads. Consequently, the systems now being sought should help to automate many subtasks of the processes in data selection and information classification for decision making and to optimize, through proper human engineering, command performance.

It should be expected that a new type of information display should utilize predetermined actions for preconceived circumstances which can be stored in memory matrices or in instantaneously available function banks of the data processing. Therefore, there is a need for a display that will enable a human operator to make decisions in a time-compressed environment.*

The solution should not be some of the present day displays with more and better trimmings, but should be unique in its approach to free the operator's mind from work which the machine can perform better and faster. This will leave his mental faculties available for functions where the machine falls short of human capabilities; however, unplanned operator interruptions require a very sophisticated computer-driven display. Such a problem will be described later with a few examples to which cybernetic principles are applied. The Pragmatoscope designed by the present writer deals in a novel way with the basic problems.

The development of complex systems requires almost in every case the interdisciplinary team effort of a number of specialists for producing the necessary multidisciplinary ideas. In the development of the Pragmatoscope, besides the system theorist or cybernetician, a position occupied by the present writer, there was need for specialists in the fields of statistics, biophysics, tactics, logistics, computers, instrumentation, sensors (radar electronics, etc.), optics, human factors, engineering and industrial designing. It is the system specialist's task to analyze the problem and farm out the sub-tasks to specialists, then synthesize their results into a functional system.

The word Pragmatoscope, from pragmatic or pragmatism, was coined as a convenient project title. It implies the testing of "truth," as a guide to action.

The Pragmatoscope represents a system and equipment which enable man to utilize a dynamic information flux, many times surpassing the perception rate* of the human mind, for the purpose of forming fast decisions. The equipment is a visual display, which analyzes facts and breaks through the barrier created by the limited perception rate of the human mind. The most critical factors in the perception of the symbols of the display are memory matching and value assessment. Basically the Pragmatoscope creates a bridge over these time-consuming mental processes.

The purpose for designing the Pragmatoscope was to provide a device with which a large number and a wide variety of external environmental dynamic signals, which are acquired in a continuous flux, can be manipulated. In it the telemetered information is optimized as to the receptor utilization of the human component in the man-machine system and as to the most suitable coding for the decision-making process of the brain.

It is a well known fact in psychology that the human sense organs have a minimum threshold; if the stimulus intensity is below this limit, no sensation is perceived. The sense organs have also an upper limit or saturation point, above which, and in conformity with information theories, no further amount of information can be conveyed to the brain in a specified unit of time. However, if one or more sense modalities* are saturated, but the rest of the sense organs still show considerable channel permeability,* the brain will handle the information by priority which it has established by past experience. In information displays generally, only one sense modality is utilized, leaving the others idle, whereas the Pragmatoscope is planned to utilize a variety of sense organs, singularly or in groups, to enable the human brain to use a high density information flux at different attention levels thereby enabling man to make decisions with minimum effort. This should delay fatigue and keep the brain in good performance for a prolonged time, which is a cybernetic requirement for this most important component of the man-machine system.

The Pragmatoscope is in essence an information-processing and display system which is combined with an integrated command module. The outstanding aspect of the Pragmatoscope is that it displays "capabilities." This term is referred to here in its technological connotation.

A decision is always the precursor of a temporal-spatial active or passive function. Every decision function is composed of dependent variables which can also be termed "capabilities." In most display systems there is a variety of symbols associated with the real world facts and/or values they represent. In contrast to this, the symbols in the Pragmatoscope primarily are displaying interacting capabilities. This fact relieves the brain of the time-consuming task of assessing values to exhibited facts and combining the values into capabilities, a process which constitutes the temporal bottleneck in decision-making.

There are visual information displays developed which are very effectively replacing the exhibiting of raw data by the visual easily apperceivable results of processed data. Such are, for instance, the Contact Analog* and the Tunnel Display.* Both of these sub-systems, however, have their limitation. They are designed to assist a pilot of a high performance vehicle in making decisions for guiding the aircraft, mostly for landing.

Machine-man-machine-man systems, to aid in the making of decisions, as the SAGE system,* were developed as stop-gap measures to bridge the chasm between the overwhelming mass of data obtained by today's highly efficient data-retrieval systems and the inadequate display systems, which were not perfectly human engineered for decision-making purposes. To have a number of persons selecting collectively data from the information flux has many shortcomings, such as the long time delay, the unpredictable reliability of the operators' value judgments in their variable state of mind, etc.

Such a multi-man system is almost as bad as a commander keeping up with a vertical combat status display where soldiers are climbing up and down on ladders to move and paste symbols on a glass pane, or on a battleship where the skipper is informed by the CIC (Combat Information Center) that a nuclear missile is approaching and will hit about 2,000 feet starboard. Walking up and down on the bridge, the CO (Commanding Officer) tells his adjutant, "Full right rudder." The adjutant says, "Aye, aye, sir, full right rudder" and down the chute (or by phone) he calls, "Full right rudder." Up comes the confirmation, "Aye, aye, sir, full right rudder" and the officer calls to the midshipman, "Full right rudder," but, of course, by that time there is no rudder nor midshipman.

Therefore, the CO of a future task force (which will be composed of a single ship) will operate a Pragmatoscope and will not have to wait for the information from the CIC to reach him, nor will he have to wait until his command decision arrives at the origin of the actuating human transfer function, because he will always see what is happening, how long it will take to happen, what he can do about it, and then do it himself.

The prerequisite for this, however, is that the pattern of command operation must be changed in a revolutionary way: the vice-admiral cannot walk up and down on the bridge but must sit and be wired by a number of bionic devices which may be implanted subcutaneously or otherwise. This is necessary to provide a closer interrelationship with his machine partner and also to monitor the efficiency with which he is performing his duties. If he becomes fatigued, he no longer is a predictable component of the system and would not be able to satisfy his machine partner's requirements; thus he must be replaced by his alternate until he recovers and again becomes a useful component of the system.

The argument that many persons will operate more effectively if under great stress is irrelevant, because the Pragmatoscope is measuring the human component's dynamic performance regardless of the factors which bring it about.

INFORMATION ACQUISITION

Before we describe the general operation of the Pragmatoscope, the coupling and monitoring of the human component in the system should be discussed briefly.

The first question is whether the human sensory receptors have sufficient sensitivity and the necessary band-width for matching the requirements of the machine.

For an efficient cybernetic coupling of man and an information display, one should utilize the superb system for the human visual perception, its interwoven feedback loops and component sophistication.

Although the human eye is a long way up the evolution-ladder from that of a frog, which cannot really "see" a motionless object, man is not different in this respect. Once the human eye has focused on a target, the muscular control system oscillates the eyeballs constantly, rendering every object in permanent motion, at least relative to the axis of the eye, providing a continuously varying contrast change over the retinal elements and producing a signal which can be quantified by the rods and cones,* thus rendering intelligible information. This parameter is not utilized in the Pragmatoscope. However, an interesting aspect of the Pragmatoscope is the cybernetic utilization of color vision, whereby the "metameric match phenomenon" is utilized. These terms refer to the experience of two lights having entirely different spectral compositions but evoking in the eye the same color sensation. Such lights are called metamers.

This is not the place to discuss the biophysics of color vision, but it should be mentioned that the state-of-the-art derived from innumerable color vision hypotheses is centered around the over 160-year-old, three-dimensional photoreception theory of T. Young and the almost 100-year-old opponent-process signal theory of E. Herring. Let us look at them briefly.

It can be said that there are essentially three different types of photo-sensitive elements in the retina, and their signals are combined in the visual process into three opponent-process signals, namely, white-black, yellow-blue, and red-green. One of the colors of each pair is apperceived when the signal is positive and the other color when the signal is negative. This concept is also called the "stage" theory, and one of the common color television systems operates on this basis. Through three filters, the image is separated into red, green and blue pictures which are viewed by three TV cameras. For each image element, separate red, green, and blue signals are generated. In a mixing network, these signals are combined into "opponent-process" signals.

In the Pragmatoscope, these electrical signals can be biased by meaningful information, and thus one can influence the color and hue of the symbols on the information display. By selecting the proper shades, chromaticity and luminosity of the color symbols, one can vary the value impression of the information without need for the brain to analyze consciously, evaluate and then synthesize the meaning of the symbols.

Furthermore, metamer spectrum combinations can be utilized by matching some types of information which come from different sources but which may be redundant or immaterial. These signals can be color-coded in such a manner that in proper combination with others they will awaken the same color sensation in the human eye; thus they do not add to the information burden of the decision-making process of the brain.

Therefore, there is no need for intermediary human brains to discriminate, select or delete symbols, as in the SAGE system, regardless of the number of bits in the display. This circumstance not only accelerates the man-machine coupling, but also makes the process more reliable because all information is available in the computer's memory, although it is displayed only in the amount which can be utilized for human decision-making. If time permits and there is reason for it, the operator may interrogate the computer concerning the type and numbers of information which have generated a given symbol.

There is a remote possibility, and a somewhat exotic one, to utilize also the dermo-optical sense in man. Research in this field of sensation is still in the embryonic state, but the reality of color discrimination through the skin of the fingers has been established. Extensive work and consequent results are published, especially by Russian investigators. A semantic remark, however, may be in order; namely, that these investigators refer to a "tactile" sensation whereas one would think that tactile stimuli are perceived by mechano-receptors.* Much more information is needed in this field, which should not be too difficult to obtain because, the popular press notwithstanding, the Russian skin is not different from ours. The chance to extend the human perception range into the infrared part of the electromagnetic spectrum which may be utilized for communication purposes is worthy of our pursuit.

Let us now turn to a general aspect of the operation of the Pragmatoscope. It is a frequent and typical pattern in combat situations, when the commanding officer and his staff are in the process of making decisions, that the CO, having arrived at the conclusion, will turn to his colleague with the words, "What do you say, George?" What he is really doing is testing for validity. He does not need additional information from his staff to arrive at a decision because he has already made it. Yet, subconsciously, he is not sure that his decision is the right one.

Therefore, he is matching it with that of others who arrived at their decisions by the same information. If two or more decisions are congruent or similar, then the accuracy of the CO's decision is greatly enhanced. Let it be mentioned here that if a heterogeneous group arrives at the same answer from the same input information, the accuracy of the decision can be considered as enhanced. In case of a homogeneous group, however, the decision under the same conditions must be considered as an "agreement," which does not reduce the probability of a systematic error.

The use of two systems of Pragmatoscopes simultaneously, called duplexed operations, is advisable to insure the integrity of such complex systems as is the Pragmatoscope because, no matter how great is the reliability, or mean-time between failure of a system, malfunction may occur either in the machine or in the human component.

The hands and feet of the operator of the Pragmatoscope are occupied by pedals, throttles, etc., to perform combat command actions, but he can flash, for a short period, onto his display the decision of his alternates, with voice control, by simply uttering a code such as "George."

In case of fast decisions, such quality assurance of his results may not always be possible. But in the duplexed mode, the Pragmatoscope would operate similarly to the output assurance procedures of critical space system computers. Therein the reliability is increased by more computers performing the same operations and voting on the result-equations which do not match. Such "voting" of machines is a highly reliable procedure.

INFORMATION DISPLAY

Those interested in cybernetics and its practical applications are probably also interested in some of the technical details which are applied to cybernetic devices. Therefore, some technological aspects should be included here pertinent to the Helvey Pragmatoscope as he designed it in 1960. If the reader is not interested and wishes to switch to the next section of this chapter, he can do so without the loss of continuity.

In general terms, one can state that the real-time* and delayed-time* information are processed in the system by selecting the important data, combining them with predetermined factors, then converting the mostly digital information into display symbols.

Symbol conversion can be performed by various techniques.

Two systems especially would give great elasticity to a wide variety of visual symbols. One is with the use of electro-luminescent lamps; the other is the application of a number of superimposed, transparent, flat-face TV tubes with tangential electron guns. A new technique is under development which permits in the same tube the use of an array of electron guns which are activated by a fast rotary switch and a phosphor with appropriate characteristics as for latency, after-image, color, etc.

Unfortunately, we are not taught in school to read and write fluently binary or other than decimal or alpha-numeric digits. Therefore, it is essential that the real-time information, which comes mostly in binary coding, should be translated directly into a dynamic display of decimal figures if these are necessary for the Pragmatoscope display. The electro-luminescent lamps, called EL-PC panels, are useful also to convert decimal information and translate it into a visual display. They lend themselves well for "and," "or," "nor," and other types of logic elements.* Complex visual information, with a high density of fast changing symbols, can be achieved by using high resolution crossed grid panels with 50 or more lines per inch. These can be viewed by TV cameras and the signal fed through the multiplexer and linearizer into the display translator. In spite of its sophistication, this device is, of course, extremely primitive as compared with the discrimination and resolution capacity of the human eye with its 100 million receptor elements.

This type of system can have also a highly important priority coding "selector" which is activated automatically as soon as the linearizer receives more than a critical amount of information flux, namely, about 40-50 bits per second. This "selector" will, at first, analyze identical types of information with reference to their locale on the display. Should it find similar symbols close to each other, then it will, instead of deleting some of them, depending on its instructions, change the size, shape or hue of the symbol, thus rendering the information in a form which is better coded for the discrimination of human sense modalities. In other words, the transferred information content of the component symbol is simply added to the system-capability symbol or system-threat symbol.

Another coding technique is also utilized for displaying reliability without the need for the brain to compute values consciously and willfully. This is achieved by making the symbols flash with a frequency of 2 to 25 cps. The lower the reliability, the lower the frequency. By very high reliability, due to flicker fusion, the operator will see the symbol as permanent as long as it has significance and is displayed. When additional information is flowing through the linearizer, a low reliability symbol may become more reliable; thus, the flicker frequency will increase, providing information which the brain will accept in an effortless fashion, as in the example of peripheral vision. In the effort to exhibit the largest number of symbols without overloading the display, the Pragmatoscope could show different types of symbols which will be "on" for one second and "off" for two seconds. During the "off" time, other symbols can be presented with similar frequency. This technique enables the brain of the operator to utilize a larger amount of symbols for useful decision-making. If the "off" time is prolonged, these "peripheral after-images" will fade below usefulness. Although considerable research and design work has to be done for perfecting the Pragmatoscope, no break-throughs are required for its operational integrity.

THE SYSTEMS APPROACH

To promote a systems approach by synthesis, the Pragmatoscope can recall temporal events and compress time manyfold, thus permitting the observation of prolonged causal effects. Furthermore, the Pragmatoscope can also dilate time by playing back, in slow motion, events, thus making fast events with short duration available for detailed analysis. One can also instruct the Pragmatoscope to recycle a given phase of operation lasting a considerable time, such as 15 to 20 minutes. In a period of inactivity, the Pragmatoscope will recycle the same events over and over until significant information enters the computer. This will override the recycling instruction.

The general operation of the cybernetic system of the Pragmatoscope can be considered as a hierarchy of process capabilities. The primitive components of the system are the human mental and anthropometric capabilities and the logic and functional capabilities of the artifact. Their capabilities are organized into more and more sophisticated higher-order capabilities, which receive their amplifying factors through the feedback of an open loop information channel. The intelligence of both man and machine is utilized to manipulate symbols and concepts for organizing and executing processes with the aid of human comprehension and problem solution.

The basic idea of augmenting human intelligence, by coupling man with artifacts and enhancing his sensory-mental-motor functions, is not new. More than twenty-five years ago Vannevar Bush described this process.† The Pragmatoscope can be considered a novel form of application of these principles.

The artifact Pragmatoscope may be regarded as partially a finite automation or a set of Turing machines* which permit the utilization of intuition, whereby it is accepted that for these aspects no *a priori* formal proof is available.

In the development of the Pragmatoscope, it is essential to design its network so as to be self-organizing, error-correcting, and reliable even with unreliable components. The information theories and cybernetics can cope with these requirements.

As indicated before, we are mentioning here a few examples where the sophistication of the Pragmatoscope is advisable. Unfortunately, as in so many practical applications of theoretical findings, the final prototype is reached in developmental steps. This is a very time-consuming, wasteful process, and economically it is seldom justified. However, life, people and circumstances do not always favor the theorists.

Therefore, the systems described below do not utilize all theoretically sound parameters of the Pragmatoscope. However, in order to promote general system research, the applied principles and some of the technological details are described here. The examples are the Missile Range Safety System, the Anti-Missile Missile System, and a Naval Combat Command System. The theoretical aspects, very similar in all three examples, will be discussed in the Range Safety System; the other systems will be discussed only in their specific mode of operation.

THE MISSILE RANGE SAFETY SYSTEM

To explain the Range Safety System and its suitability for Pragmatoscope application, one must first consider the responsibility of the Range Safety Officer (RSO) and the data-processing within the system. Essentially the work profile of the Range Safety Officer consists of:

1.   information acquisition;

† Bush, V. As We May Think, *Atlantic Monthly,* July, 1945.

2.   information processing;
3.   human decision-making aided by cybernetics; and
4.   control function with "true time" feedback informa-
     tion.

From the time the Test Center Commander accepts a missile
flight schedule, the RSO is responsible for the safety of persons
and property anywhere in the range of activity of the missile. The
duration of the authority of the RSO depends on the mission and
the type of vehicles. In case of a ballistic missile after burn-out,
which may take a few seconds or as much as 5 to 6 minutes, his
responsibilities are over. Suborbital flights he will monitor all the
way, but orbital and deep spacecraft will remain under his
command only until they go into orbit and again from the start of
the re-entry maneuver.

At any time prior to missile launch, the Range Safety Officer
may hold or cancel the firing. After firing he must make a decision
whether the missile is to proceed as planned, have its thrust
terminated, be directed on a different course (for aerodynamic
missiles) or be destroyed. In the case of ballistic missiles, he may
take action only until thrust termination, except for destruct.

In performing his duties, the Range Safety Officer must
consider two extremes, and he must make a decision between
these. First, he must protect personnel and property which could
conceivably be damaged by the missile. Secondly, he must not
modify or terminate the "good" missile flight prematurely because
of the expenses involved and the value of the data which can be
obtained every second of flight-time. Therefore, the decision to
destroy a missile requires accurate and timely information, careful
consideration, and alert action.

The data upon which the Range Safety Officer makes his
decision may be divided into three parts: (a) information pertain-
ing to the missile and range equipment prior to launch, (b) launch
data, (c) information obtained during flight.

If the information from these three areas were always 100
percent accurate and completely comprehensive, the chances of
incorrect decision would be very low; however, there is always the
possibility that the extrapolation of data obtained for operational

prediction could present erroneous results. Since the information is not entirely complete and accurate, the tolerance of prediction is broadened and the possibility of an incorrect decision is increased. Therefore, systems employed for range safety must provide the best data obtainable and deliver this data to the Range Safety Officer in the most understandable and accurate form.

Information which is available to the Range Safety Officer prior to launching is presented to him over a fairly long period. Even in the future, the information should be available for many hours and possibly even days prior to actual launch. At present, the Range Safety Officer begins a study sometimes several weeks before a launching. During this period he has to have available such data as the calculated flight path of the missile, missile idiosyncrasies, launching equipment status, land masses, personnel and property within or near the missile danger zone as well as status of the range safety equipment. During the beginning of the period, data input density is fairly low; however, during count-down the data input quantity rises sharply and the probability of data accuracy increases.

Launch information is defined here as that information which is available to the Range Safety Officer from the time the missile is fired until automatic programming of the missile begins. During this period the missile, if operating satisfactorily, is usually rising vertically. If the direction of the missile's movement reverses, it is a duty of the Range Safety Officer to destroy the missile, thereby spreading the impact over a large area and lessening the chances of a ground explosion. If the missile veers off course, it may endanger surrounding installations and personnel and property outside the launch facility. The data during this phase therefore must be accurate, rapid, and clearly presented to the Range Safety Officer. Data must also be presented in much more detail than during other portions of the flight, since missile movement during the launch period is very small compared to the overall travel.

Once a ballistic missile "programs,"* it is possible to begin impact prediction. This impact prediction, together with previously assembled information, present position of the missile and the status of range equipment, is now available to the Range Safety Officer. The accuracy of the information presented during this period is variable. Impact prediction accuracy increases during the flight of the missile, since a large portion of the prediction is dependent upon past performance. Present missile position is determined by sensing devices. The fidelity of the information is dependent on the accuracy of these devices and the distance between the devices and the missile. With these inherent system deficiences, it is essential to permit as little degradation as possible when transferring the collected information to the Range Safety Officer for evaluation. This position of the system dynamics lends itself particularly to cybernetic considerations.

At any time during the period in which the Range Safety Officer is responsible for the missile, it is frequently necessary that he analyze all available data. This includes the information presently being transmitted to him as well as past information. He must assimilate this data as rapidly as is humanly possible and be prepared to make accurate decisions. It is evident, therefore, that the system which transmits the data to the Range Safety Officer must be as accurate, rapid and reliable as practical and consistent with the operational capabilities of the Range Safety Officer.

At present, aside from routine forms of communications such as conversation, written reports, etc., the Range Safety Officer has electronic communication facilities which allow contact, at his discretion, with the firing area, range officials, data collection facilities and auxiliary control locations. The communication equipment associated with these links consists of standard telephone networks, a special RSO telephone (green phone) and an intercom system; the latter is integrated into the system to provide for all operational and backup communication facilities.

Presently from a master countdown system the Range Safety Officer has available digital information for operating countdown indicators. Other firing data sources include a lift-off indicator and television facilities for observation of the firing pad and the missile during programming.

Several range instrumentation systems are now employed for missile tracking. These include radar, optical and other systems. The output from all these systems accepts the instrumentation outputs, and performs impact predictions which are made available to the RSO system. Calculations are performed to indicate which data source is the best at any one time, and this source is used in the impact prediction. "On track" status signals are also provided to the RSO system by special sensors.

In order for the Range Safety Officer to digest the vast quantity of incoming information, a comprehensive display system is provided which makes possible the selection and display of pertinent data. During missile launching the television system is used to generate two displays: one showing the firing pad and the other the missile as it travels vertically and *programs.* After the missile is in flight, the display system shows to the RSO the missile path relative to a ground plane and to elevation profile. The scales employed for these presentations may be set to provide the best trade-off between reading accuracy, tracking speed, and reference interchange.

In order for the Range Safety Officer to make a decision to continue the flight, to destruct or to extinguish thrust, it is necessary for him to know where the missile will impact if at that specific instance he terminates the flight. This knowledge is obtained by using the available impact prediction signals and presenting them on display similar to that used for "present position" data.

The Range Safety Officer is equipped with control devices which allow him to arm and to destroy the missile. As a back-up, he is also provided supervisory control for remotely destroying a missile from a down-range station.

To insure the operational readiness of all equipment used in the Range Safety Officer System, status indicators and special testing devices are presently provided. Indicators also inform the Range Safety Officer of equipment malfunctions while the equipment is in operation.

The following additional equipment is provided to assist, as much as possible, the Range Safety Officer in the performance of this mission:

a. Secondary reference preparation facility for processing of map and chart data into a simplified form.

b. Recording facility for preparation of permanent flight records for use in post-flight analysis.

c. Interval timer and in-flight elapsed time indicator.

In the Range Safety Officer System, as well as in any other system, the designer is faced with conditions other than those imposed by technical requirements. These requirements which are established primarily by the design philosophy may be termed "boundary conditions." By analyzing first the technical requirements and then imposing on them the boundary conditions, it is possible to design a system meeting all requirements. For the purpose of this presentation, reliability, human factors and maintainability will not be considered as boundary conditions but will be referred to as "Design Considerations."

In the Range Safety Officer System there are several conditions which greatly affect system design. One of these is the application of the RSO console design which has been accomplished by the Atlantic Missile Range. This console was designed in detail and in accordance with the requirements of the Range Safety Officer whose input and output requirements as well as configuration have been established. It is now necessary to fit this sub-system into the overall system. Preliminary design has also been accomplished on the Data Control Console; however, this is not considered a design boundary but rather a suggested approach from which the designer may deviate as necessary in consideration of the overall system objectives.

The human sense organs as components of the System are fairly sensitive signal detectors, and in some cases will surpass the sensitivity of the machine. The overall precision of the human operator, however, is low as compared with that of the machine. For instance, in problems of analog-addition and analog-multiplication, a simple computer would have an accuracy of at least one order of magnitude better than that of the human operator. This is also the case in other linear control functions; as a differentiator in estimating velocity, the human is the weak link in the system. Since analog integration simultaneously involves two factors, namely, multiplication and time judgment, the human mind will fall far short of approaching the efficiency of the machine. The severe limitation of the human link in the man-machine loop is his limited band-width. The human organism is basically a single channel, single process device. Due to the inaccuracies of the human link in a closed loop man-machine system, the human must be regarded as a source of noise. The level of this noise is quite significant and must be considered in the design of every higher order man-machine system. Also the gain control capability of the human link is very poor, and it may vary from day to day and from individual to individual. The gain variability of the human can be as high as 30 db* as compared with a stable mechanical or electronic system. This shortcoming can be somewhat overcome by placing feedback loops around the operator which can be combined with some high-pass antibias network.*

Beside the non-linear gain control, innumerable dependent and independent variables in the human sub-system dynamics cannot be expressed, at the present time, in digitalized form; therefore, it is necessary that a homeostatic mechanism be inserted between man and machine.

As long as the artifact is highly automated, its interface with the human link will be sensitive to variations in the human performance, and maximum systems reliability will be attained.

It can be safely stated that a well-matched system, due to its reliability, would yield a more satisfactory output in the long range, even if it operates at a somewhat lower performance level, than a mis-matched system. One of the reasons is that the mis-match of sub-systems puts undue stress on the same sub-systems which consequently would fail before their expected mean-time-between-failure. Furthermore, a chain of incompatibilities could arise.

To alleviate such variable incompatibilities, the total system should be made elastic enough to adapt to the peculiar non-linear instability of man. In other words, a given reaction speed or a certain type of vigilance may be expected from the human sub-system for an optimum system performance; but, due to fatigue or other reasons, the human link may not perform according to the requirements. In such case, the system should automatically lower its demand in its sensitive parameters. In such case, the system's performance would experience a decrease, of course, and such adaptation would have its limits to maintain system integrity. However, within such limits, a feedback of information on the time-dependent actual human performance, which is directed into the automatic system-control, would have a desirable effect on the overall performance.

The prerequisite for such a feedback of human performance

is the gaining of much more knowledge on this matter. This in itself is a difficult problem; because human performance is a composite of many factors, and a realistic value of it can be established only if the human individual in question is tested. However, the test procedure, by using conventional psycho-physical performance tests, will influence critically the status of the human body and mind and will, therefore, interfere with optimization.

In other words, if very high performance is demanded from a man-machine system, due to the unpredictable instability of the human performance, information on the operational integrity of the human link cannot be ascertained beyond a certain limit and by means of telemetry of physiological parameters. It becomes necessary to use frequent performance tests which, using presently known techniques, will interfere with the performance of the individual in two ways: (1) It will be time consuming because during the testing the utility of the human component in the system is lost and (2) all test procedures are also energy consuming; thus the tests add in an unpredictable manner to the decreasing performance of the human link.

A solution seems to be available, if the artifact has a sensor which matches constantly its own performance with that of the human link. If a failure sensing device does not indicate mechanical breakdown, then the reason for lower output is the temporary performance decrease of the human link. In such case, the feedback loop should lower the total system's performance to a level where the human temporary capability is adequate for efficient operation.

For instance, to give a primitive example, if the control or steering of a vehicle requires a certain angular correction limit for a given speed, but the excursions of the directional axis become greater than the predetermined safe maximum, then the feedback loop should automatically reduce the speed of the vehicle to a limit where the sensed axis-excursion is tolerable. In case of more complicated systems, more sophisticated automatic mechanisms are required which, however, are well within the frame of present technology.

It can be considered as primitive the way the Central Control of present day launching operates. In lieu of proper cybernetic design and engineering features, dozens of highly trained, expensive but non-linear human components are inserted into the system. The present argument is that they have to "keep an eye" on the indicators of various sub-systems—truly a "horse and buggy" type operation.

One can, of course, argue that there are many ways to deal with non-linearities, such as operating on derivative feedback terms,* etc., and that we should employ non-linearities to get the maximum use of the man in the system. But why use a human component where his capability is marginal? On the other hand, the automation of the machine in the Range Safety System is quite limited according to the present state-of-the-art without the Pragmatoscope, and the human link makes positive contributions with his learned skills and experience.

In the foregoing, the human link in the man-machine loop has been regarded rather mechanistically as a true component of the machine system. The picture would not be complete, however, if the human link were not viewed from the psycho-physical and psycho-physiological points of view. This special treatment is fully justified if one is regarding the uniqueness of the organism.

The Range Safety Officer's prime duty is to evaluate certain visual stimuli coming from an information display and to make a vital decision under predetermined circumstances. During the missile flight, the Range Safety Officer decides whether the flight profile matches the expected pattern or if the dynamic event on the display crosses the predetermined danger profiles, called destruct lines.

Before we treat the man-machine system of the missile-flight command or the range-safety task from a cybernetic point of view, let us briefly justify why it needs such treatment.

The Missile Flight Commander's or Range Safety Officer's mission is a typical partially closed loop, man-machine system. The loop is open during the flight of the missile, but it is closed in the event the Range Safety Officer has to destroy the vehicle.

The flight command or the range-safety task of the Range Safety Officer of, e.g., the Atlantic Missile Range, is a complex system in which a large number of real-time and delayed-time data are made available to a human link in the system for decision and control functions. There are also typical feedback loops within the machine, and between man and machine in the system. All of this clearly indicates that a cybernetic approach to the optimization of control and communication functions is warranted.

The sense organs of the human will perceive a relatively weak signal only if he is paying attention to it. The problems involved in the human vigilance are, however, manifold. Provision has to be made, therefore, to include warning signals strong enough to draw, under all circumstances, the attention of the human operator to the incoming signal. Mention should be made here of the recently designed Tele-Summoner* of the present writer, which is an automatic tactile signaling device. Its signal will generate the so-called exogen need.* The proper perception and utilization of the displayed signal and the efficient transfer functions through the machine depend on a large number of external and internal factors. The decision and the subsequent mechanical or vocal command will also be influenced by them.

ASSIMILATION OF DISPLAY
INFORMATION AND DECISION MAKING

There are a large number of intrinsic and extrinsic factors which influence visual perception. These factors vary in importance, and they shall be considered accordingly.

Since the process of decision making is, in the case of the Range Safety Officer, strongly related to the displayed information, these should be considered together. Basically, the task of the Range Safety Officer in the system is to observe an information display which is generated by signals coming from a number of sensors. The information is obtained partially through a real-time and partially through a delayed-time communication system, and the sensors are far from being perfect. Therefore, the Range Safety Officer cannot evaluate the display symbols according to predetermined scale, but he must also take those factors which he has memorized, as well as the countdown, into consideration. This is by far the strongest argument for utilization of the Range Safety Officer in a decision-making capacity. If the data acquisition and data handling were perfect, there would be no need for a Range Safety Officer, because a computer could be constructed which would be able to compare the incoming information with precomputed and predetermined data. In the event of excess deviation, the computer could generate the necessary destruct signals. Due to the large number of variables which cannot be predetermined and because of the need of logical induction, the presence of the human mind in the Range Safety System becomes a necessity.

In an information display, there is a "number of symbols versus time" function which, depending on various psychological and physiological parameters, will determine the operational limit of the observer of the display. This limit varies greatly from person to person. The percepted image of the information display is matched in the mind of the operator against learned data which are stored in his memory. This matching is a "GO"–"NO GO" type superimposition on memorized elements, but certain favorable or unfavorable values are attached to the pairs, which have technical and emotional vectors. These values are mentally summarized and translated by the mind into a matrix pattern. This matrix then represents the decision. The decision in the form of its matrix or integral is meaningless until it is solved or, in other words, is again translated into certain symbols with well-defined and learned information contents. It can be proven that the operational speed of any sense organ is great, and so is the mental translation of the decision into mental symbol images or even psychomotor functions. The bottleneck seems to be the search for matching and the establishment of associated values. This function may be localized between the thalamus and certain cortical regions of the brain. This matching and evaluating process is, in many cases, conscious and impulsive. Therefore, the role of accomplishment must be, and is in most cases, also conscious and impulsive, although sometimes it occurs as a reflex action and in the subconscious. At any rate, due to prolonged preparation and especially to repetition of partial countdowns, considerable energy is spent in the process, and all forms of fatigue will occur—which tend to reduce the efficiency of the subject. This is why optimum environmental conditions must be provided for the Range Safety Officer.

This is further emphasized by the fact that during decision-making, and especially if the decision is of severe consequence, the dynamic flow of signals to the brain is quite limited. In other words, the human mind acts like a narrow band pass filter. If someone is concentrating on making a highly relevant decision, external stimuli are competing for his attention. In order to facilitate decision-making, it is understandable that one has to minimize extraneous signals. This is particularly so in the case of the Range Safety Officer, considering the large amount of predetermined data and the status parameters of the sensors which he has to recall and consider during the flight of the missile. It has to be mentioned, however, that the predetermined variables before and during the countdown are also limited in numbers, and the Range Safety Officer must rely to some extent on the information he is gathering from the display. It can be shown in many cases that the information present is inadequate for the foundation of a terminal decision; and, if a decision is forced under such conditions, the possible error may be beyond the permissible limit.

To avoid such a situation, as much predetermined data as possible should be programmed into the flight path and impact prediction computer system. Analytical considerations have shown, however, that the amount of instruction which can be given to the computer for programming operations on the incoming messages is very limited. This limitation emphasizes again the necessity and importance of the human link.

It is obvious that the observer, or human link, must detect and evaluate the signals displayed on the information display. A number of studies on detection theory have been concerned with estimating the efficiency of the human observer as a decision maker. Among other techniques, this can be done by comparing the performance of the human observer with that of an "ideal" observer as a standard. The performance of the "ideal" observer is expressed as a ratio of the probability of detection to the probability of false alarm for different values of the so-called cut-off points, and for a given signal-to-noise ratio. This expression is based on mathematical computations that have been worked out for a number of special cases. The performance of such an ideal observer is optimum in the sense that all the information in the input is used in making the decision. The human observer is presented with the same signal and noise, and his detection and false alarm rates are measured experimentally. The human performance, which must be less or equal to that of the ideal observer, is measured by computing the amount of signal attenuation required for the "ideal" observer to yield the same performance as that of the operator. The ratio of this level to the actual signal energy is a measure of the human observer's efficiency. It is obvious that the mission of the Range Safety Officer consists of perception of visual signals, detection of these signals under "noisy" conditions, assignment of values to the perceived signals and the use of these signals for making optimum decisions.

The human operator, by observing the information display, and based on peripheral information, must continuously decide whether what he sees is "signal" or "noise."

If the probabilities for the "signal" are very much greater than the probability density for "no signal," then it is, of course, easy to make a decision and call the observation a signal. But in the case of the Range Safety Officer the probability densities are not so widely separated, yet a decision has to be made. The ratio between the probability density of "signal" versus that of "no signal" can be called the "likelihood ratio." The task of the Range Safety Officer is to find the smallest "likelihood ratio" that he will accept and still call the observation a signal. Then, all observations with a "likelihood" greater than this ratio will be called signals, and all observations with a "likelihood" less than this will be called "noise" or signal not present. This point is then called the cut-off point.

It is clearly visible that the decision theories which we are considering in connection with the Range Safety Officer's work are composed of observations, probability density functions, *a priori* probabilities and a set of values. He uses these factors to attempt an optimum decision about the observation.

It can be shown that the observer of an information display will act according to the various decision criteria described in the theory; therefore, all aspects of the decision theories will enhance the usefulness and maximum efficiency of the recommended man-machine system.

The *a priori* probabilities assigned by the man are not necessarily the true *a priori* probabilities. Instead, they represent the observer's beliefs concerning the true probabilities. They are based on his past experience, training and understanding. Obviously, the observer can decide only on the basis of subjective probabilities, unless he is provided with information about the true probabilities. The theory does not demand that the operator should have information about the true probabilities, but only that a probability for each alternative should exist. When the observer makes a decision, he is exposed then, for the first time, to the consequences of the discrepancy between his assumed probability and the true probability, since it is then that he becomes aware of errors. At this point, he finds that he does not realize correctly the unexpected values. As a result of this finding, he may modify his subjective ensemble of probabilities to correspond more closely to the true probabilities.

The ability to form likelihood ratios is assured by taking the "noise" into consideration. It can be felt intuitively, beyond the mathematical proof, that the observer will make improved decisions and make them faster if the noise level is low. The term "noise" as we have used it in the foregoing can be intrinsic or extrinsic. The intrinsic noise is generated by the very complex nervous configuration of the human organism. This is due to the fact that the human mind is unable to concentrate completely on a certain given task; a considerable part of his mental capability is constantly occupied by extraneous matters. Due to this basic characteristic of the human mind, one should not force the attention to a focal point with the complete exclusion of extraneous signals, because under such conditions the person may disregard rational facts and the task at hand, and could pursue fantasies. Certain shortcomings of the perceptual mechanism which may cause disturbing phenomena, such as positive and negative after-images or illusions, can also be called intrinsic noise.

The extrinsic noise is generated outside of the human body, and these factors can act directly upon the human sense organs or indirectly through the psycho-physiological channels. These extrinsic noises can also be called environmental stress. It is obvious from the foregoing that our design task in optimizing the man-machine system for the Range Safety Officer console must have as its main objectives reduction of the intrinsic noises to as low a level as possible and the determination of the optimum level of extrinsic noise.

It is obvious that the crucial point in the system of range safety is the decision for destruct command. Such a terminal decision is connected with, and dependent upon, individual or statistical values and events. A statistical decision problem arises when we are faced with a set of alternative possibilities. This is the case in destruct command because this simple binary function is distributed in the time dimension. Arbitrarily, we must assume that a choice must be made, and the degree of preference depends on an unknown distribution function.

All statistical decision problems are formulated with reference to a random process.

In case of the RSO, there is a finite number of chance variables. Even so, with the exception of the simplest cases, the choice of the possible decisions will be made after entering some enhancement of the probability by gathering information. This is done by taking into account observations on chance variables in a given sequence. Those decisions, which can be made only after the completion of observations, are called terminal decisions.

It is, of course, possible to make wrong decisions, but there are ways by which one can reduce them to a minimum. The choice of a decision function* is a unique solution of a terminal decision, and can be considered as inductive behavior. The main reason why a decision may be wrong is the risk which is frequently associated with the decision. For the reduction of the risk, various mathematical instruments are available. Such mathematical instruments can be utilized in a separate loop of the system, and displayed to the operator. Decision functions which minimize some average risk are the so-called Bayes solutions,* and the minimax solutions.* The latter are decision functions which minimize the maximum risk. These two solutions are closely related to each other in as much as a minimax solution is really a Bayes solution for a least favorable distribution.

It is interesting that game theories* can be very useful in the solution of risky decisions, although their application depends on the available time. A decision problem can be considered as a zero-sum two-person game* in which the two players are the "Decidor" and the mechanical-automatic part of the system.

Furthermore, the strategy of one of the players corresponds to the time distribution of certain parameters of the Range Safety System, and the strategy of the other player represents the choice of the decision function by the "Decidor." The outcome of the game could be considered as the risk, and the minimal strategy of one of the players as a Bayes solution. This would seem to justify the thought that the trend of the mechanical part of the system is to *maximize* the risk, which, of course, is the weak point in the above comparison.

There is no question about the need for extensive automation in the flight command system. However, automation should be a tool for terminal decisions, not a substitute for command.

The present thinking in flight command of space vehicles is to provide a number of staff members with individual information displays and an automatically displayed summary or status of the pertinent data which changes in the time function. In the Range Safety System a computer-generated map display is available to the human link in the control loop.

At a later date, when the space lanes will contain a relatively high density of vehicles, the available time for decisions will make it impossible to follow any chain of command. For such a situation, let us arbitrarily assume that the necessary information for a good command decision is 500 to 600 bits per second. Our data processing equipment can handle such a flux very easily, but the capacity of the human brain is about one order of magnitude less. Unfortunately, we cannot use 10 human brains to make partial decisions and correlate them into a terminal decision, if the necessary time for such a coordination is not available.

In designing the human operator as a link into an integrated data processing and control system, it is very deceiving to compare the human mind with a computer. The truth is that there are certain superficial similarities between man and computer, such as the specialized input and output components and the presence of about 10 billion neurons in the human brain resembling diodes.* The resemblance is enhanced by the "all or none" law of the neural activity, which strongly resembles the "go or no go" type of binary function of certain computer components. Furthermore, there are a large number of parallel channels and by-passes which enable the brain mechanism to perform its task even if some of its elements are not functional or if there is considerable functional noise present. There are, on the other hand, many mental activities which cannot be compared with any kind of computer activity. The major part of higher mental functions is connected with such non-computer types of systems. It is hoped that within 10 to 15 years, by which time the Pragmatoscope might be put into operation, noteworthy advancement will be achieved in our knowledge of these non-computer type mental activities.

The close interaction between man and machine in this system requires the standardization of the human link as far as this is possible. The Pragmatoscope achieves this by telemetering psycho-physical data from the operator and comparing these with a set of standards. If the operator falls below these standards, the system will apply stimuli to the operator either through his sense organs or through implanted bionic devices.* If this fails, and the operational integrity of the human component does not improve, the system will call for a new operator.

A novel feature of the Pragmatoscope is that it utilizes in a semiquantified form peripheral vision and subliminal information. However, no further design details can be given here for the Pragmatoscope, and this report is, of course, only a small segment and a survey of an extensive study on the subject.

HUMAN ENGINEERING DESIGN ASPECTS

Because in most cybernetic systems man is an integral component of the operational unit, although this is not so by definition, some of those design parameters which are important for such integration should be described here.

In general, the human engineering design aspects of the Range Safety Officer System must include:

Factors associated with

1)   the input message,
2)   the environment,
3)   human assimilation and use of display information,
4)   the work space layout, and
5)   reliability.

For proper human engineering design, one cannot omit the analysis of the types and frequencies of the messages which arrive at the center. The analysis must consider:

a)   reception of the input message,
b)   interpretation of input messages,
c)   translation of input messages, and
d)   encoding and transfer of input messages.

These phases of data handling are very critical. The manner in which the input messages arrive and how they are handled raises problems which, without proper consideration, might void the rest of the chain of messages. Thus, automatic and delayed-time data must receive priority ratings. For real-time data, the priority can be established by predetermined information which is put into instantaneously accessible function banks. For the delayed-time type information, the data handling personnel must be properly indoctrinated with a set of ground rules. Since the receiver of the input message must determine the priority of his message, problems of interpretation and translation will bear investigation. Concrete items, such as rates of message transfer, must be investigated as part of a time and motion analysis to determine the overall compatibility of the receiver tasks and the systems function.

The following factors must be carefully evaluated in the design of the information display, and the corresponding optimum values applied:

1.   Distance of the display screen from the operator
2.   Ambient illumination
3.   Line-width of the track and symbols
4.   Color of the traces and symbols
5.   Trace and symbol luminosity
6.   Symbol to background contrast
7.   The rate of the information flux

The ambient illumination should be in the neighborhood of 5 millilamberts* and should be adjustable by the Range Safety Officer. But the adjust knob should not go down to zero because enough light must be present to enable the Range Safety Officer's dark-adapted eye to see the parts of his body and the outline of the furniture. Otherwise, even within a few minutes, he might have the illusion of floating in air, which could cause vertigo, or other illusions.

The background to symbol contrast should be within the 1:3 to 1:6 ratio limits.

The Range Safety Officer's cubicle should be soundproofed. The soundproofing should not be made perfect, because complete silence is, or can be, very irritating. Yet the outside noise may distract his attention to some degree. It is better practice to completely soundproof the room and introduce controlled noise or some music in the 1-2 db level. Some random noise will also be provided by the electronic equipment in the console and the display, and by other operating personnel. The low level permanent noise is also valuable because it eliminates the possibility of a mild shock or startle which would occur from the relatively high intensity sound of the intercom system after a long silence. It can be proven that such occurrence will cause a mild seizure in many people. The recovery time can be several seconds.

In the foregoing discussion, we demonstrated the importance of proper environment for the efficient operation of the Range Safety Officer. If we analyze the environmental factors which should be taken into consideration by the design of the Range Safety Officer's work space, we arrive at the following major factors:

1. Information display characteristics
2. Illumination
3. Noise
4. Temperature
5. Bodily comfort

In order to demonstrate the complexity and the involvement of the application of cybernetic principles to complex man-machine systems, it seems necessary to go into such details as those found in this chapter. Without these theoretical and practical considerations the reader would not be able to appreciate the task at hand. To move the "story" faster we shall restrict any further "nitty-gritty" to just a few more "dat."

In the information display green and red colors will be utilized as well as black and white. Aside from the regular visual cues, peripheral visual information will be applied as secondary cues. This will provide redundance for reassurance and increase of confidence.

The ambient temperature in the RSO Operations should be 72° with 45% relative humidity, and a permanent air velocity of about 1 ft. per second. This air motion with ventilation should assure constant carbon dioxide content of the air of about .03% partial pressure.

A comfortable, well-designed padded chair of the executive type, which can swivel and recline in the usual manner, seems to be satisfactory.

In the design approach, it is recommended that there should be a convenient railing in front of the information display which the Range Safety Officer can grab during flight. This can provide subconscious reassurance and balance provided by grabbing the armrest of the Range Safety Officer's chair. With this configuration the Range Safety Officer can move to the optimum distance from the information display, depending on the visual area in which he is interested at any given instance.

The human link is an important part of the Range Safety Officer's System; and, therefore, his reliability as a component or servo system must be analyzed. This analysis will consider the capability of the human sense organs and mind with respect to the mean time to failure under the stresses which the machine is imposing on him during operation. In case of the human operator, the simple experimental failure law,

$$Sp = e^{-t/f}$$

where

Sp = probability of success
e = Naperian base
t = duration of operation
f = mean time between failures or merit

cannot be applied. A much more complex function governs the occurrence of the human error. Since many variables in this function are unknown, exact mathematical models cannot be constructed and inductive reasoning is inapplicable.

Some approximations are, however, available from experiments and previous experience. Special attention must be given to the fact that in case of the human reliability the finite cutoff points for the extreme "impossibility" and "certainty" are approached in a complex fashion.

Part of the human factors associated with system reliability is involved in the maintainability of the system. The main difference between reliability and maintainability is in the degree of dependence on human factors. Reliability is primarily a hardware characteristic. Secondarily, it is related to humans due to the possible maltreatment or abuse of the equipment. Maintainability, on the other hand, is by its very nature primarily a human function.

In the maintainability design, one must consider anthropometric and biodynamic factors as well as the factors of proper muscle coordination or dexterity. The anthropometric aspects deal with the accessibility of components with reference to the shape and dimensions of the human hand. The biodynamic considerations analyze the force vector's magnitude and direction in relation to the capability of joints and muscles to be used for a given task. If such analysis shows marginal figures, a "tool" has to be designed to extend the capability of the human organism.

It should be mentioned here that one of the strange, but necessary, aspects of reliability is that the system should be sabotage-proof. This can be achieved by various interlocks and signaling devices to protect the equipment.

In all sensitive systems, and quite emphatically in the Range Safety Officer's System, reliability must be established during the design. It cannot be overemphasized that from the preliminary design stage through the final detail design, reliability must be a major consideration. No amount of quality control, operational testing or maintenance can achieve a degree of reliability higher than that which has been designed into the system.

We do not wish to show at this time the mathematical considerations of the failure probability. However, it is safe to say that if a unit has a failure probability of 1000 (that is a reliability of 99.9%) the probability of independent failures of two such units in parallel is one in a million, giving a reliability of 99.9999%. On the other hand, it can also be shown that if the reliability of the component is 99.9%, the application of 10 components in a series will reduce the reliability to 99% and 500 components to only about 60%.

The level of component reliability required can best be illustrated by reference to automatic switching systems for telephones. American Bell Telephone System considers a failure rate of one in five million, which is 2×10^{-7}, as unsatisfactory performance. To complete a single call circuit, about a thousand relay operations are necessary. Therefore, to meet the system reliability requirements, the maximum permissible failures rate for a relay is approximately 2×10^{-10}. This in itself indicates that in the Range Safety Officer's System the required level of reliability cannot be achieved without the use of redundancy.

Considering finally the human aspects of the man-machine system reliability, we have to state that in a broad sense no system is reliable regardless of how low the failure probability may be, unless the human operator can do with it what the equipment is intended to do. Therefore, such factors as perception rate, which is about 40 to 50 bits of information per second, and reaction time of the human link, which for the simplest function is 200 to 300 milliseconds, must be taken into careful consideration.

Furthermore, for the enhancement of the reliability of the human link coupling, as well as for best efficiency, the broad spectrum capability of the human senses can be fully utilized in the design. These senses include, besides hearing and vision, tactile and kinesthetic perception.

In summary, it was intended to show the concept of an advanced man-machine system in which the human link is integrated with the artifact in a wide variety of interfaces, with a large number of feed-back, control, self-regulating open and closed loops.

The intention of this chapter is also to spotlight a number of important characteristics of the human link and those of the artifact in the system and to point out areas for general systems research.

5.
BIONIC SLEEP CONTROL
IN ASTRONAUTS

The man-machine symbiosis in astronautic mission-profiles requires that the human component should be adaptive to various sleep-wakefulness cycles which are different from normal rhythm. Therefore, it became necessary to design a bionic device which would couple the members of the crew through a computer, or rather a control system directly to the temporal-operational universe* of the spacecraft.

In this chapter, the biophysical and psychophysical aspects of the self-organizing wakefulness center in man are treated in some detail because the mechanism of sleep is far from being well understood. The chapter mentions the efforts of the international scientific community as well as the results of the writer's own experiments.

The present writer's philosophy in attacking this problem is that there exists a natural self-organizing sleep mechanism, which is based on a complex biochemical and biophysical information flux as part of a complex control and feedback system. Even if one does not fully understand this mechanism, an axiomatic approach may yield enough algorithms which can be the basis of a model, and thus an example for biocybernetics.

It is of major concern for the system analysts of space vehicles to establish the criteria of operational integrity of the man-machine system. One of the great problems in putting the human element into mechanisms with prolonged linear functions is the human cyclic behavior. Among many inherited and acquired periodic traits, the rest-wakefulness cycle requires prime attention.

It has become obvious from astronautical task analyses that the terrestrial indoctrination of eight hours sleep and sixteen hours wakefulness will not be possible to maintain during many types of space missions. Yet, this habit is very firmly indoctrinated. The acquisition of this behavioral pattern dates back to the imprint stage* because it was manifest in the mother. The infant has experienced early that any interference with this pattern meets with the covert or overt hostility of its environment. This adjustment was reinforced later by the cosmic diurnal cycle and thus developed into the social attitude of day-work and night-rest of most of mankind.

It has been shown in many studies of human efficiency that, depending on the activity, fatigue or boredom will bring about a significant decrease in performance. There are drops in efficiency in the mid-morning and mid-afternoon, which established the "coffee break" system as a social behavioral pattern. Not only the wakeful state has such fluctuations, but also sleep shows periodic phenomena. However, in astronautics, without the social work pattern and cosmic cycles as we know them on earth, it will be more advantageous to fall into a cycle different from the 8/16 hours rhythm.

It has been suggested that for prolonged translunar missions a four hours wakefulness, four hours sleep cycle should be adopted. Such a cycle seems proper for the work profile expected for certain space missions. The diversity of the duty cycle at various types of missions will, however, require an even more flexible pattern, where the astronauts may need variable sleep-wakefulness periods which would best fit the mission. This proposition, however, will meet with difficulties due to the strong habituation of the 8/16 hours rhythm. This is why artificially induced and well controlled sleep has become an important problem. The goal is a bionic device which initiates healthy sleep and which can be controlled by the requirements of the organism and the vehicle.

There is a considerable amount of literature available on the physiology and biophysics of sleep; however, little is known about artificial sleep. Yet the problem of sleep is quite important in the human factors of astronautics, because of the need for maintenance of high efficiency of the man-machine system. Sleep is the best long-range remedy for all variants of fatigue, which must be · reduced to a minimum, since certain space tasks are quite intolerant of poor performance.

Besides this recovery from fatigue, sleep may be used for sleep learning or reinforcement of learned information. This latter aspect will become significant in aiding recall of little used data which, however, may be needed suddenly without permitting the necessary time for consulting books or tapes.

BIOLOGY OF SLEEP

To show an example for the practical application of a bionic system of sleep, it is not essential to go in depth into the biology of sleep. However, because sleep is still an unsolved physiological phenomenon, some details are mentioned here. Although sleep is a most basic bodily function, amazingly little is known of its fundamental mechanism. This is true in spite of the virtually thousands of scientific papers dealing with the subject. Therefore, a brief review is given here presenting some of the more important aspects.

Consciousness vs. Sleep.

Even the terminology of consciousness and sleep is quite confusing. There is no space here, of course, to discuss the semantic subtleties of the difference between consciousness and wakefulness. In rough approximation, it can be stated, however, that during consciousness the organism is meaningfully perceiving environmental stimuli and is capable of decision making and of activating psychomotor functions.

In general there are three essential aspects of sleep:

1) the quality or depth of sleep,
2) the quantity or duration of sleep, and
3) the rhythm of sleep.

Maybe the greatest difficulty in sleep research is the measurement of the depth of sleep. A quantitative evaluation of this factor is most pertinent because of the wide spectrum between drowsiness and coma. The physiological and psychological aspects of sleep depend greatly on the state of sleep. There are a number of measurements proposed for the determination of depth of sleep.

One system uses the numbers 1 to 4 to indicate states of sleep; another uses the letters A to G with intermediates denoted by a (+) or (-) sign. Still others refer to slow, rapid or no eye movements which are associated with states of sleep. Fair quantitative information can be provided, with good reproducibility, using electroencephalograms (EEG), which will be discussed later. Furthermore, a number of stimulus gradients were applied for establishing depth-of-sleep curves. Auditory, visual, tactile and pain sensations were used, however, with little reliability. Stupor and hibernation, although these stages can be considered as extremes of sleep, will not be discussed in this chapter.

The duration of sleep is strongly dependent on the age of the person. In adults an average of 7.5 hours sleep per 24 hours seems to be a basic human trait because it holds for all races of Homo Sapiens, at least for those who live in temperate zones.

The sleep-wakefulness rhythm is anchored very firmly in the human physiology. Body temperature changes and other physiological collaterals of sleep do not change readily even after prolonged training. In a test, after many weeks of training, subjects of 12-hour sleep cycles reported no overt discomfort, but their body temperature rhythm remained corresponding to the former 8/16 hours cycle.

Meteorological factors, which have such a profound influence on sleep, are meaningless for astronautics due to the controlled environment of the closed ecological system of the crew compartment. Cosmic cycles may still have bearing on sleep in the space crew compartment, but research data on this are incomplete.

Anatomy of Sleep.

Among many investigators who have contributed to the anatomy of sleep, M. Jouvet* is outstanding. According to Jouvet, two different neurophysiological systems are controlling sleep:

1)	the telencephalic* activity, which has an inhibitory effect on the ascending reticular system and originates in the cortex of the cerebral hemispheres.
2)	the rhombencephalic* phase, which has an inhibitory connection to the limbic system in the midbrain and the reticular cells in the pons.* These reticular cells are responsible for the maintenance of alert wakefulness if stimulated from peripheral sense organs.

Of course, since Aristotle, many thinkers and physicians and other related professionals have developed various theories of sleep, none of which were satisfactory.

Some of these theories are relating sleep to the circulation in the brain; others to temporary synaptic disconnects* due to amoeboid motion* of neuroglia cells.* Again, others are advocating that there is an undetected sleep center in the brain which is responsible for the loss of consciousness. The theories of the accumulation of a specific metabolite called "sleep poison," or hypnotoxin, as well as the instinct theory of sleep were explored with insufficient results.

The fact of the matter is that the mechanism of sleep is not yet well understood.

Physiology of Sleep. Sleep-Feeding Relations.

As indicated above, sleep has a profound influence on many physiological parameters. They are so numerous that only a very few can be mentioned here.

The pH and the blood sugar content of the blood do not change significantly during sleep. There is a slight change in the calcium equilibrium in the body fluids during sleep, but no other noteworthy alternation has been observed during sleep. The pulse-rate, as expected, decreases in the sleeping person; and, as an extreme, a rate of 45, two-thirds of normal, has been observed. The blood pressure in the body also decreases, with drops of 20 to 30 points, or about 15 percent of its pressure in wakefulness. These figures may account for the anemia in the brain during sleep.

What is interesting is that adrenalin, which causes a strong increase in blood pressure in the wakeful person, fails to do so during sleep.

The symptom of snoring is not considered a pathological condition, and it does not influence sleep except for those persons who have to share the environs of the snorer. Respiration is altered by sleep, but the reports on the details are quite conflicting. Digestion in its biochemical phase is not greatly influenced by sleep. Some glandular change has been reported, such as the accumulation of bromine in the anterior lobe of the pituitary gland. The change in body temperature is not considered to be related directly to sleep but to the lack of muscular activity.

Psychology of Sleep. Dreaming.
Considerable information is now available concerning dreaming. The results are quite far-reaching and show that dreaming is a necessary physiological-psychological activity. During the dreaming phase, the blood pressure is generally higher and the variability greater than during other phases of sleep. It is considered, however, that the blood pressure might not be as specific a concomitant of sleep as other factors, rather that it might be due to emotional changes during dreaming.

In a spacecraft, where extensive physical exercise is unlikely, the maintenance of the sleep state, which is accompanied by rapid eye movements and which contains the subjective experience of dreaming, is an important factor of life support. It should be mentioned, however, that the correlation of eye movement in sleep with dreaming is not precisely established, and further research is indicated.

The functional integrity of the astronauts is related also to sleep control from a psychiatric point of view. It seems that dreams and hallucinations are brought about by a similar mechanism; thus, psychosis and dreams are related mental processes. From this point of view, it is essential to monitor carefully the sleep pattern of the astronauts, because sleep disturbances are characteristic for the onset of functional psychosis. It should be pointed out, however, that the electroencephalogram and the eye-movement pattern are similar in the normal and the schizophrenic persons; thus, such telemetered information to ground control would not give significant indication of schizophrenia occurring in the astronaut. It was found also that dreaming and the associated rapid eye movements correspond to

EEG of low voltage and without the so-called sleep spindles. Between the dream periods are distinct intervals of cyclic pattern. At these times there are no eye movements, and the EEG is entirely different. However, cyclic changes corresponding to dream experience are not restricted to symptoms occurring in the EEG, but significant changes are manifest in muscle tone, frequency and depth of respiration, skin resistance, blood pressure, etc. These symptoms are easily measured and lend themselves well to telemetry back to earth.

The rapid eye movements are not continuous during dreaming, but the 4-5 dream experiences per night are normally uninterrupted for longer or shorter times, depending on the person's age. For the age limit of 20 to 30 years, the total time of dreaming during 7-8 hours of sleep is one hour and 30 minutes, with amazingly little individual variation, and a dream occurs about every 90 minutes.

For the mental hygiene of the astronauts it seems important that they should have good, wholesome dreams every 5-6 hours to avoid "day dreams" or "hallucinations." According to theoreticians in this field, dreams are instinctual-drive discharge processes in the id,* the significance of which has been demonstrated by dream deprivation experiments. These experiments lead to hallucinations. Obviously, the dream-sleep cycles are governed by quite deep-seated physiological, innate mechanisms. Freud called dreams "safety valves." If these valves are closed, the pressure for discharge mounts until the "dreams" occur during wakeful periods. The process of dreaming is called by Jouvet "rhombencephalic phase," which seems to be somewhat cumbersome nomenclature, but has anatomic significance.

It is believed that dreaming is also connected with neurohumoral secretion.* Thus, there might be developed in the future a biochemistry of dreaming, but it is likely that the understanding of dreams will need purely psychological interpretation.

There are certain similarities between dreaming and the effects of sensory deprivation. This seems to indicate that dreaming is in fact independent from sleep but is related to the relative absence of environmental stimuli which are essential for wakefulness and the various aspects of adaptive behavior.

Although we cannot enter here into the detailed psychodynamics of sleep, it seems that for the proper functioning of astronauts on long missions we will have to control not only the sleep cycle, but we will have to manipulate also the quality and the duration of dreams.

Sleep Deprivation.
Chronic disturbances in indoctrinated sleep cycles may lead to anomalies of waking experience and behavior. It can easily lead to psychosis. If muscular activities are excluded, it is impossible to deprive a normal person of sleep for longer than two days.

Prolonged sleeplessness causes irritability, irrationality and hallucinations. It causes also marked and increasing performance decrease. There is a stage or state of mind where the concept of wakefulness becomes transitory to sleep.

Psychophysics of Sleep. EEG.
If one is looking at a flickering light, rhythmic signals appear on the EEG which change with the flicker frequency. This indicates that those signals were generated in the visual projection area of the brain. It is significant that the flicker is generally accompanied by sensation of motion and patterns. The action potential which is concomitant with every biophysical or dynamic activity of every cell is manifest also in brain function.

The best understood pattern of electroencephalograms is that of sleep. It enables us to clearly distinguish between the various stages or levels of sleep and arousal.

The total picture is, however, not as simple as indicated here and extensive literature is available for the interpretation of further and complex details.

SLEEP CONTROL

The human mechanism has an apparent shortcoming as compared to a bionic device, namely that it cannot be switched "on" or "off" as needed. Of course, there are bodily activities such as recovery from fatigue, etc., which require the proper functioning of the body during a non-conscious period. This occurs, however, at a lower metabolic rate, although it can be said that during dreaming sleep we are more intensely alive than in the conscious or waking existence. But there are a number of ways which permit a certain limited control of sleep. They are briefly mentioned below.

Training and Indoctrination.

It is possible that by prolonged training most individuals will acquire a four/four hourly rhythm. It must be expected, however, that such terrestrial training may initiate neuroses, because the forced rhythmic behavior may not coincide with the long established physiological "clock" mechanism. This condition will be further aggravated by the weak environmental signals which will reach the person even in his confinement and which tend to reinforce the deeply embedded original pattern. The astronaut will be especially susceptible to these weak signals as a consequence of the stress of sensory deprivation caused by the confinement in the space compartment. Of course, the simulation of certain nocturnal noise, to which the urban population is acclimated, may be used to override the weak diurnal noises. However, this method may not be sufficient to provide sleep.

Drugs.

The use of hypnotics must be discarded, because our present inventory does not contain a compound or mixture which would initiate sleep rapidly; nor does the compound have a well defined four hours of duration and permit a quick arousal without any after-effects.

There are drugs, the hypnotica, which facilitate sleep, and narcotica, which cause in many people irresistible and deep stupor. However, hypnotica, if administered in larger quantities, will cause a state called narcosis, or, if the product is applied through respiration, anesthesia.

Hypnosis. Post-hypnotic Suggestion.

This method cannot be recommended because of the limited duration of its effect. It is thinkable that a combined post-hypnotic and auto-suggestion technique which would utilize an artificial clue, such as a tape recording, may work for a longer time, but this method has not been demonstrated to be reliable.

Beyond the aforementioned practical space applications, it is significant that the below mentioned technique of electronically induced sleep could contribute to our understanding of the various hypnotic states. From a few experiments it seems also that this technique will have therapeutic values inasmuch as those neurotic patients who resist hypnotherapy could be brought into a state of consciousness where their excitation and hostility are reduced enough to make them responsive to hypnotism.

Visual and Audio Stimuli.

It is a well known fact that certain rhythmic photic stimuli or monotonous audio signals have the tendency of hypnotic sleep induction. The effects of flickering light have been under study for about 200 years, and they have brought us quite close to being able to disrupt consciousness and thus manipulate the onset of sleep. Previous reports have indicated that the limit of the results was a slight hypnotic effect, with drowsiness and occasionally with unpleasant side effects. The impairment of cognition by flickering light has also been described.

Electrical Current.

Japanese and Russian reports, together with the research of the present writer, which he has performed in the past several years, suggest that the solution to the problem of sleep control of the astronauts may lie in the area of cyclic electronic stimulation of a so far unknown resonance area in the brain, which reduces cognition and willful activities.

It is known from research here and abroad that electrical stimuli of a certain frequency, if applied to the brain, will cause drowsiness or sleep.

The electrical influence of consciousness can be subdivided into three distinctly different types:

1)   electroshock
2)   electronarcosis
3)   electrosleep

Electroshock was used extensively in certain mental diseases such as schizophrenia and sometimes to supplement prefrontal lobotomy.* Lately, it is applied less frequently. The effect of the relatively high current density has the danger of artificially causing a seizure, with temporary blocking of respiration. This type is applied only to psychotic patients and does not concern us here.

Electronarcosis, also called electroanesthesia, is a modified subseizure, or electronically induced loss of consciousness, without drastic effect on respiration. However, convulsions are frequent and the application of muscle relaxants is indicated. Sometimes the extreme rise of blood pressure puts this technique into the dangerous category and should be applied only by expert hands. In spite of this, electronarcosis has definitely a place in astronautics.

Although the character traits of astronauts are as carefully determined as possible, under many months or years of lasting space stress, some psychosis may occur. For instance, in the reaction to sensory deprivation, of which there will be many in space, there is the defense against a break with reality. Such persons experiencing sensory deprivation will be greatly prone to hallucinations and delusions. Many reports indicate that electronarcosis can be successfully applied to alleviate such conditions.

Since electronarcosis has a hypnotic effect, which brings the body to the reflexless stage, it can easily be applied in case of medical emergency. Anesthesia could be in short supply in space, but electricity will always be available.

CONCLUSION AND FUTURE DEVELOPMENTS

Man spends about one-third of his lifetime sleeping. This in itself indicates the significance of this state for the physiological and psychological homeostasis of a normal person.

Unfortunately, the sleep-pattern of man does not always match the requirement of our modern and sophisticated socio-technocratic life. Therefore, recently it became necessary to study the mechanism of sleep. The aim of such investigation is, besides the scientific information, the desire to manipulate sleep. What is known, in essence, is the fact that monotonous repetition of audio or visual stimuli has frequently induced sleep in a number of subjects. This effect has a number of dependent variables, such as frequency spectrum, environmental factors and variables of certain mental states.

In addition to the condition of insomnia, this problem received impetus by the design of the work profile of long-range space missions. Because of the sometimes highly taxing performance requirements, it is imperative that the astronaut fall into restful sleep at any regular or irregular intervals. Of course, drugs which cause drowsiness or have other side effects are out of the question.

It has been confirmed by the writer that sinusoidal electrical stimuli to the optic nerve in the 9 to 12 cps range will bring about sleep in most subjects within minutes. The current applied is below the sensory threshold of the skin, and the sleep-homeostasis is fair, provided the arousal level is not exceeded. In other words, the effect shows stability against overriding stimuli. The created flicker seems to dominate, if applied long enough, even over otherwise strong arousing audio stimuli such as soft jazz music.

The biophysical or psychophysical problem of sleep control has a broad spectrum for experimentation. Large numbers of individual experiments have to be carried out for statistical evaluation of the results. They will demonstrate the considerations which are needed if one deals with a single factor of a complex system.

It does not seem far-fetched to expect that within a relatively short time man will develop equipment which may be pre-set to alter his biological clock of sleep.

The time might even come when implanted bionic devices will control sleep and wakefulness. They could be governed by biophysical or biochemical symptoms of fatigue; this would eliminate the overtaxing of our physiology and prevent the exposing of our psyche to undue stress. Such a condition will significantly increase the life expectancy of mankind. We could live 150 or 200 years, taking even into consideration the lack of regeneration of our cardiac tissue.

Of course, when such time comes, our activity pattern will be greatly changed. You may feel a prickle on your skin above the implanted bionic device. This could signify: "You are working too hard, better go to bed—because in five minutes I will make you sleep." On the other hand, after two hours it might wake you, and if you choose to stay in bed it will sense the reduced rate of respiration and circulation and will deliver continuous mild electric shocks which signify: "You are lazy. I know you are well rested. Get up and do whatever you want to do." And this is not science fiction; it seems that a good old standby, the alarm clock, is about to go out of fashion.

6.
SOME CYBERNETIC ASPECTS
OF HISTORY

The fantastic technological developments of the past 100 years and the economic affluence which is spreading somewhat unevenly throughout the world have brought about a new world view which is pregnant with anxiety and meaninglessness.

We see our system parameters converge toward Nietsche's Nihilism, which he predicted more than 80 years ago. Up to that time our society was based on purely physical images, as defined by Kant. However, the behavioral and social sciences are contributing more and more to the present organismic revolution. Life appears as an accidental outcome of physical processes, with the human mind as the epiphenomenon.* In the same way, in the current theories of evolution, the living world is a product of probability and random mutations. The human personality is considered in the theory of psychoanalysis a chance product of nature, through gene-interactions and accidental events from the imprint stage to maturity.

Lately, however, some people are looking toward a world of diminishing entropy. If the validity of such a concept can be verified, it will profoundly alter scientific thought and practical applications. The milestones of this era are the emergence of new sciences, such as cybernetics, systems analysis, bionics, etc.

112

Contemporary psychology, as a science of man, is full of contradictory theories. Behavioral engineering is frequently based on rat experiments. The incompetent philosophy of existentialism is totally unable to deal with true human situations; and other approaches, such as computer models of cognitive processes, provide obviously untenable robot models for human behavior. So far, robotic concepts, although disapproved of by many overtly and covertly, remain the dominant view in psychological theory and in research and engineering.

The main argument, namely the stimulus-response model, which is the basis of behavior in instinct, and in conditioned and non-conditioned reflexes, is now under attack. This is the case in the classical unconditioned stimuli of Pavlov, the operant conditioning by reinforcement according to Skinner or early childhood experience according to Freud. It seems unreasonable and difficult to accept that the verbal behavior of children is generated by the same mechanism as the reward results of bar-pressing by rats and pigeons.

Another seemingly incomplete principle is environmentalism, according to which behavior and personality are formed by the exo-environment. Watson, the founder of behaviorism, once said "Give me a group of children and by conditioning I will make them into doctors, lawyers, beggars, or thieves." This would mean that the human brain is a computer which can be programmed at will and to any degree; and this would indicate that all men are born not only with equal rights but with equal capabilities. This presently popular trend is the reason why in our society such a great emphasis is put on mental health; and this is why such significant funds are being spent to bring back the mentally ill and the criminal into society.

The Freudian principle of the homeostasis of basic mental functions appears to be a lame horse. The statement that "all that is needed is promiscuity: give people sexual release from tension and they will be satisfied and normal," is beyond doubt incorrect. Another strong, but luckily outdated, principle is operant economy: Children should learn only as much as absolutely necessary to become business executives or other upper level professionals, otherwise tension will be created in them, their personalities will be warped, and they will become unhappy and maladjusted.

The obvious shortcoming of all this is that the stimulus-response scheme omits such human activities as play, exploratory behavior and creativity. Pavlovian environmentalism is untenable even in dogs. Furthermore, life, with all its essential open loops, is typically a dynamic, non-linear, semi-steady state equilibrium, which means that its *homeostasis* is aimed at a continuous change; thus, it is rather *homeodynamism.*

Juvenile delinquency committed for fun, psychopathology due to inactivity, and skyrocketing numbers of mental cases due to overprotection by the social system clearly demonstrate that adaptation, conformity, adjustment and social equilibrium are not the road to the survival or to our culture and civilization. It can be shown that cultural endeavors, such as the intrinsic value of Michelangelo's or da Vinci's works, do not follow economic or utilitarian principles.

If environmental stresses would eventually simply give way to homeostasis and not also promote development in an ever-decreasing entropy pattern, then man would have never developed from the amoeba. The amoeba is doubtless the most successful homeostatic biological system, which survived billions of years in an unimaginable changing and always hostile environment. But obviously the pattern of life is not a leisurely assimilation to convenient prototypes.

This leads to the concept of an active personality system, which is already supported by a number of new sciences, such as developmental psychology of Piaget and Werner, the ego psychology, the personality theories of Allport and Maslow, the existential psychology and the revolution in education. Today we are under the impression that a new model of man has become necessary. This model emphasizes such organismic functions as creativity, individual basic differences, non-utilitarian biological values beyond survival and subsistence, which are innate in the active organism. The re-orientation of psychology brings about the great interest in the systems approach and cybernetics, because it is unreasonable to assume that creative or cultural accomplishment like the composing of the ninth symphony by Beethoven or the painting of the murals in the Sistine Chapel can be regarded as "response to stimuli," "gratification of biological needs" or "re-establishment of homeostasis." Human endeavors are full of violations of the "basic drive" for satisfying biological needs.

The cognitive processes must also be regarded in a new light. This is based on the circumstance that man does not simply record and react to information from the environment, as a photographic film, but that by complex, cybernetic data processing he assembles in a creative manner his universe, that is, the symbolic image of it.

The new image of man replaces the robot concept by the systems approach. Hereby it emphasizes the endogen activity instead of exogen reactivity, recognizes the essential differences between human cultural activity and the behavior of lower mammals, etc. This will eventually lead to a re-evaluation of problems of education, training, and also psychotherapy. One may regard this also as the newest upswing of the pendulum between dualism and monism, not in the religious but rather in the cultural sense. The systems concept is particularly applicable to humanity as a whole and to all of its subsets. This courses the social sciences away from the classical atomistic concept, which neglects relations, and also from the trend which is called "social physics." Research in this field is extensive and quite successful. Problems like population growth, the armaments race, deadly conflicts, automobile traffic, etc., yield to the systems approach; even the spreading of rumor can be explained and to a degree predicted by a set of differential equations. From the smallest social group, the family, through structured higher echelons like nations or power groups, or unstructured groups like rioters, to international relations, the systems theories are applicable. This indicates the possibility of an analytical systems explanation and eventual modeling of the history of mankind. Although this seems now to be a formidable task, the successful practical application of cybernetics and other systems sciences in business, engineering and international politics has demonstrated that complex, dynamic processes lend themselves to such treatment.

Theoretical history demonstrates that culture, tradition and language enable man, and man only, to consciously be aware of his history. The question which interests many is whether history has laws. If so, how can it be modeled? The usual scientific technique of nomothesis—the establishment of laws which are based on objective fact and which are repeatable and factual—does not work with history, because history does not repeat itself. Therefore, it is ideographic, that is, it describes a singular event which seems unique. However a number of very capable thinkers, like Hegel, Marx, Spengler, Toynbee, etc., have maintained that historic events can not be just accidental, and that human behavior, which results in history, must follow certain laws or programs. This has been verified on a small scale in mortality rates and demographic statistics, prediction of voting behavior and the methods of advertising. Also, econometrics is a system oriented tool which, in mathematical economy, does not always concern itself with physical entities. Information theory, decision theory, game theory, etc., deal with those behavioral elements where classical science is not applicable. But certain regularity can be observed in such cultural patterns as the arts and their development, which always show a primitive stage, then various stages of maturity and eventual dissolution. This is also true in the cases of various civilizations, which are recognized as following intrinsic, specific and organizational laws. So far only laws of "micro-history" are accepted, which are restricted to small social groups, short intervals and restricted space. "Macro-history" is still a virgin territory, but explorers are already pioneering in it. The proof of the pudding is in the building of models and their operationalism. In achieving this, it is easy to fall into the pit of over-simplification. One can argue that by reducing the complexity, one may be able to construct a model and then test it for validity. The difficulty is multiplied by the cybernetic nature of cultures and civilizations. They also have uncertain limits with uncertain characteristics; even their number or existence is uncertain. Yet, small socio-cultural systems have a definite life cycle, which is recognizable in most cases, in spite of all the feedback loops and interactions, which seem impossible—but are a fact.

The greatest hurdle in modeling history seems to be semantics. Even the meaning of the concept of culture is disputed. Kroeber has collected (in 1952) 160 different definitions for it. The notions of the various professions, such as anthropology, history, etc., are most incongruent. To Spengler, the philosopher, culture is a dynamic, self-evolving entity; while, to anthropologists, a culture of Australian bushmen, or that of ancient Greece or the modern West, belongs to a stream of amorphous humanity with environment-induced ripples or waves.

Strangely, such verbal differences are often more than purely semantic problems, they have political significance. In Canada there is a distinct "biculturalism," whatever that term means. In the U.N., the term "culture" is handled on anthropological principles, resulting in endless confusion. Somewhat facetiously, it should be mentioned that a manufacturing plant is a system which shows some characteristics of an organism, but so does the botanist's "plant." The bivalence of the industrial and botanical "plant" is easy to define. This metaphor is well understood in the French language, where a commercial firm, a professional association and the postal service are all called *"organisme."* It is interesting how modern experts such as Toynbee and especially Spengler in *The Decline of the West* agree that in spite of our dynamic, skyrocketing technology and science, bolstered to a great extent by military need, we live in cultural decay and a state of impending catastrophe.

The dominance of mass man, the suppression of the individual by a dictator or a militant minority, the cult of status symbols and sectarianism, the war between a decreasing number of superstates, are part of the socio-cultural syndrome of the second half of the 20th century.

It appears that most people with creative ability are disenchanted, or have lost interest for intellectual and spiritual activities. Let us quote Rotovcseff, the famous historian of the last epoch of the Russian Empire: "Remarkable the psychological change in those classes of society which had been up till then the creators of culture. Their creative power and creative energies dry up; men grow weary and lose interest in creation and cease to value it, they are disenchanted; their effort is no longer an effort toward a creative ideal for the benefit of humanity, their minds are occupied either with material interests, or with ideals not connected with life on earth and realized elsewhere."

Contrary to the doom which caused many civilizations and cultures of the past to perish, we are able to see hope of permanence for our epoch. The decline in the past was caused by an inherent vulnerability of the strongly spiritually oriented, advanced society, which succumbed to another subset of humanity, which was more viable and aggressive, because its survival depended on aggressiveness. However, due to present technological advances and more intimate knowledge in the communication sciences, the present trend is more holistic, encompassing all of mankind. We seem to be heading for a global culture. Today the carrying of the torch of culture is not the privilege of a select few, as in times past. Intercontinental interactions are becoming more and more numerous. African tribal cultural parameters have become essential parts of present-day Western civilization. No doubt, the radio is "spoiling" the cultural pattern of the Australian bushman as well as that of the Indios in the Andes.

As von Bertalanffy has remarked: "The Decline of the West" is not a prophecy but an accomplished fact. The European culture in the past 1000 years, which produced Gothic cathedrals and the works of Leonardo da Vinci, Michelangelo, Shakespeare, Goethe, Newton, Gallileo, Kant, Marx and Einstein is dead, and it cannot be revived by any means available to us today.

At present we are faced with the reality of technological, international mass civilization of global scope. The power of struggle, which is typical for every transition, whether in small sets as a company management, a larger one as in the Negro movement or an even larger one as in the case of the super-states, is pregnant with violence. A systems analyst understands it and even expects it as a natural overshoot in the search for equilibrium. If our technological capability in nuclear power, and soon in intelligent machines, does not destroy with its viability our vulnerable society, then one can expect the elimination of global differences, because they will become trivial in view of the magnificence of a global terrestrial culture. In the meantime, we can look forward to a glorious past.

7.
SOME CYBERNETIC ASPECTS
OF EUGENICS

The betterment of man is an old problem. Starting with the Egyptian Pharaohs, all ages have recognized that from certain points of view men are not constructed equally. All kinds of natural and man-made distinctions were created, resulting in various segregations not only in the Western civilization, but also in other parts of the world such as India, China, and Africa.

Essentially, in all cases the basic, mostly unidentified and subconsciously perceived reason was to avoid the enlargement of the human gene-pool, which would bring about hybrids with undesired hereditary traits—undesired primarily from the viewpoints of the present society.

In all ages, some of the nations have performed eugenics in a way which was morally unacceptable for other people, such as the custom of the Spartans to kill weak children, a procedure which found repetition in a more or less similar manner in some primitive people.

Another attempt in eugenics was the trend of restricted marriage by the royalty. The eugenic value of such inbreeding seldom brought about the intended results and was then abused for power politics. Because of the ignorant use of genetic principles for eugenics, human failures became numerous, and this custom will soon be only of historic interest. An attempt was made by Hitler to achieve planned eugenics. However, the applied method not only lacked scientific basis, but was also morally unacceptable to the people. At this time the psychological makeup of humans does not tolerate artificial breeding of man, supervised and directed by the state.

The scientific aspects of eugenics have multi-dimensional complexity. One of the complex variables in one of the dimensions is the strong heterogeneity of the inheritable traits of mankind.

The second complex variable is philosophical and automatic in nature, and deals with the so-far undefined parameters which should become predominant in the amelioration of the human race. Sociology and anthropology are in the analytical phase of the study of what constitute the desirable human traits in the various parts of the earth. As long as this aspect of eugenics is not better founded, and its spacial-temporal factors established in quantifiable terms, haphazard hybridization or eugenics engineering through chromosome manipulation is quite meaningless.

It is obvious that a system which is as complex as eugenics lends itself well to a cybernetic approach. What is considered a virtue in the Congo is considered highly undesirable in Ireland, and there may not exist a uniform set of hereditary parameters which are applicable to all subsets of the human system. However, it can be expected that with the rapid growth of the communication and the transportation technologies, such differences of the social-ethical vectors become unstable in the time domain and will slowly fade away. Those persons, however, who are presently interested in eugenics will not want to wait a couple of centuries until right and wrong are accepted uniformly throughout humanity. Therefore, these persons will have to tailor their efforts in eugenics to relatively small segments of mankind. Such efforts should be promoted because they will be invaluable proving-grounds for the feasibility of eugenics.

There seems to be emerging in the technologically advanced countries a trend which will provide a natural means for eugenics which is acceptable for everyone, even at this time. The field which will provide the scientific platform for planned eugenics is astronautics.

Long-range space flight will always be an expensive under-taking. Regardless of whether it is organized by the government or by private enterprises, only carefully selected persons will be admitted to the crew. They will always be the physically, emotionally and mentally most suitable individuals for the stressful task of space flight. These select groups will at first inhabit some of the planets of our sun, whereby they will live in artificial, closed ecological systems. As the technology of astronautics advances into flights beyond the solar system, a new selection will be made from these "Space-experienced" groups to pilot the new spacecraft. Assuming that they will arrive alive on a habitable planet of a solar system, they will colonize it, and their offspring will have the improved qualities of the pre-selected gene-pool. It can be expected, however, that the genotypic* as well as the phenotypic* characteristics of such a population will not be stable. Due to mutations, the originally superior chromosome map may deteriorate. However, the survival characteristics, brought about by the environmental stress of the alien surroundings, will soon eliminate the backlash. After this the colony will stabilize and will plan to explore and conquer further habitable planets.

The human resources of the colony will not be abundant by the time they are emotionally and psychologically ready for the next trip. Therefore, the new adventure will greatly tax the human resources of the colony, because the crew of the ship must be again most carefully selected to improve the probability for the accomplishment of the mission.

It is quite unrealistic to assume that vehicle speeds of a third of that of light would bring about a traffic between these different star colonies which could contribute to the hybridization of the population. Consequently, as a human species moves further and further out into space, it automatically performs eugenics. How far such undirected selection can go is unimaginable due to our very poor knowledge of topographic genetics and the related molecular biology. If artifical gene-manipulation will not be achieved, although some improvement in the techniques of this science can be expected, then the further we go from earth, the more super-men we will find—that is, *become.*

Relatively soon, maybe in a couple of thousand years, this breed of man will develop into a sub-species which we may call Homo Coelorum, or the man of the skies. It is reasonable to expect that within 50,000 years a major part of our galaxy will be explored and, wherever possible, inhabited. By this time, due to the evolutionary trend of speciation, as a consequence of the varied stresses of the exo-environment of these planets, as well as the subsequent changes in the endo-environment* of these men, many useful character traits of Homo Sapiens will be bred out of these super-men. Eventually a regressive hybridization with a primitive earth-man will become necessary to avoid degeneration and to maintain hybrid vigor. This, however, will be very complicated and difficult to achieve, because it must be done backwards along the eugenic pathway, since the humanoids from the remote parts of the galaxy will not breed with earth-man due to genetic and physical incompatibility, and a new dimension in cybernetics will be necessary to solve that problem.

It can be seen that even astronautics will not provide for the ultimate perfection of mankind, but at least it will ensure a long trend upwards.

8.
SOME CYBERNETIC ASPECTS
OF HUMAN HABITATION

One of the characteristics of cybernetic systems is their tendency to be "self-organizing," due to the feedback and feed-forward structure of a number of information channels, all of which have some sort of a control function at their termination. Such systems exert a characteristic resistance against any change caused by some stress from within or from without the system; this behavior is called "Homeostasis." Another aspect of cybernetics is that it can be applied to *all types of interactions,* whether they occur between living or non-living objects or forces, or any combination thereof.

It becomes obvious, even from this very sketchy and incomplete description, that cybernetics is ideally suited to the study of many aspects of human habitation. There is nothing more "interdisciplinary" than the interactions between society and its environment, and there is probably no other system which is more complex than modern man and his habitat.

Due to the multidimensional, complex structure of such an open ecological system as human habitation, with its continuous flow of materials and energy in and out of the system, there is a hierarchy of dynamic parameters which attract a wide variety of specialists, such as planners, developers, architects, sociologists, and students of ekistics (the science of human habitation) as well as specialists in transportation and communication problems and many others. All these learned persons have become more and more interested in urban and regional affairs and vigorously apply their chosen special fields of interest, with some overlap in a few other special scientific areas.

Unfortunately, the problem of urban crisis does not lend itself to a solution by any specialist, or even teams of specialists, but requires the broad horizon of generalists with intimate knowledge of cybernetics and its mathematical tools. Mathematical techniques, such as optimization of non-stationary random events, information theories, linear and non-linear programming and the input-output statistics developed by Leontieff,* with his advanced version of multidimensional matrices and their second and third order interactions, are necessary for the construction of mathematical models of human habitation. Without these, realistic planning and high cost-effectiveness in development are not possible, and remain guesswork or at best an art but not a science. It is essential that with the aid of such tools and other methods all, or at least most, of the parameters of human habitation should be quantified or their heuristic trends established, because then and only then will we be able to utilize intelligently the billions of bits of information which, of course, have to be amassed in the meantime in the storage of an advanced high-speed digital computer with futuristic logic capability. Great steps toward the solution of social problems can be expected as breakthroughs in approximating human emotions and ethnic characteristics for computer input became available. These techniques require, of course, much further development, but this is only a matter of time. With these data in a computer, the recalled information can be passed through a digital-to-analog converter and be used to construct a dynamic mathematical model of specific human habitation. This will provide high-accuracy forecasting of the operational integrity of planned habitation for social subsets, and will be an invaluable tool for "quality control" in urban and regional development.

Admittedly, this technique is very difficult and complicated—but so is man and his milieu. Very few planners, developers or architects are also mathematicians familiar with the above mentioned modern mathematical techniques. Therefore, they will tend to oversimplify the task at hand and hope that their design will fall in the "ball-park" of requirements. They often suggest that the inevitable correction to their design errors will be made as they occur. There are very seldom fatal errors in the design of structures or hardware because if, for instance, a structural beam for a building is computed with first approximation of the utility load and with first order interactions, the designer adds 200, 300 or sometimes even 500 percent to the dimension of that member as, what he terms, a "safety factor." Such generally accepted methods are really a cover-up for lack of data in dealing with second and third order interactions of numerous feedback loops and large sets of parameters, which provide the requisite variety. Thus, such a system is accessible to cybernetic considerations. Due to the mentioned over-simplification, the design is frequently very remote from being isomorph; that is, identical with the design goal. Therefore, in many cases "urban renewal" becomes a bottomless barrel for funds, and so-called model cities are often models only due to the ambiguity of this term.

Credit should be given to the many sincere and knowledge-able efforts in the advancement of the state-of-the-art of human habitation, which have promoted and solved many problems and eliminated many deleterious symptoms which plague the urban environment. However, the time has come for the application of all achievements and the know-how which man has developed in hardware and software for the exploration and control of terrestrial and celestial environment to the improvement of his habitation.

It seems beyond doubt that the so-called urban ills are directly related to the size and the density of the population, with its unidirectional migration trend toward the cities. Dynamic demography, which studies the causes of population movements, is fast becoming a reputable science which, however, is still in its analytical stage. Thus, it can recognize and explain certain parameters in population movements, but it is far from providing reasonable control functions. If the difficulties in the cities arise because of the population pressure toward metropolitan and megalopolitan areas, maybe a solution exists in "de-urbanization."

This term is considered a "dirty word" in certain quarters, because so much capital and political power have "vested interests" in the large cities that any suggestion which may curtail further urbanization is considered a threat to their interests.

But these persons and/or organizations should have the vision to realize that a planned de-urbanization, by using and promoting today's and tomorrow's habitation-technology, will bring about a heretofore unheard-of wealth and governmental power. They should recognize that such a system and its dynamism will remain for a long time in an unsteady state, which can provide rewards which surpass the most ambitious dreams of those who invest funds or efforts in *happy human living.* The forcing functions in dynamic demography, with all its vectors directed toward the city or metropolis, do not coincide with the basic hedonistic, that is, basic pleasure-seeking, characteristics of people. Therefore, functional and emotional stresses develop which are the real cause of the difficulties in the large cities. And this is why the elimination of *individual* symptoms will not be able to solve the total urban crisis.

Also, the assumption that a well designed city will satisfy all men of different ethnic, social, economic and cultural levels is not based on fact. The homeostatic or self-maintaining trend of small subsets of human society is so deeply rooted that artificial mixing cannot satisfy the stability criteria for a long time. Here is where second and third order interactions become critical.

This country will graduate from its universities in the next few years about 1000 planners per year. How many of these will be educated with a view to the interactions between tomorrow's technology and the hedonistic pattern of ethnically, culturally and sociologically different people? How many of the academic community, who are teaching these prospective planners, are willing to make the change from what they have learned, which is now obsolete, to what their successors will learn, which is not yet in any textbook? How long until the revolution in education will reach the next generation of planners, so that their models will become truly congruent with all aspects of man and his milieu? Would it not be wise to incorporate cybernetics into the curriculum? To do so will definitely improve the competence of our planners.

9.
SOME CYBERNETIC ASPECTS
OF POLITICS

It is found quite frequently in the Russian technical literature the dogmatic statement that cybernetics is one of the scientific expressions of dialectical materialism. It is claimed that cybernetics is singularly applicable to the Marxist philosophy.

What seems to be evident is that Marxian socialism aims at a classless society through a forced transformation of the "old" system (capitalism, feudalism, imperialism, etc.). But also in a democracy a classless society can come about through an abundant production of sophisticated intelligent machines, which eventually will become symbiotic with man and will bring about a classless society, at least as far as economic stratification of the average person is concerned. The Communist cyberneticians are approaching this aim so differently from the societal cyberneticians in the democracies that only some of the mathematical operations of their theoretical model building show some similarities. Of course, the Soviet cyberneticians are developing intelligent machines and in advance of the Western technologies; but, conforming to the party line, their aim is socio-political. The first attribute of intelligent machines in the Soviet socialism is to overcome the atavistic social imprints in the population, which is coupled with the restriction of the free pursuance of human desires and the regimenting of human activities. This is justified by the misleading socialistic argument that the method is unselfish and aimed at the willful integration of the social group of mankind into an optimal and highly unified system, which will bring eventually happiness to all. Therefore, this tool, this goal, should be enough incentive to serve with devotion and satisfaction the communist doctrine and the policy of the Party—which has the wisdom to lead the people toward the goal. Unfortunately, the human masses do not have the intelligence to see the light and their best road to happiness, because they are indoctrinated by the capitalists and imperialists. Therefore, they need a strong governing patronage for their own good. This is, of course, a typical mistake, which can easily occur if a synthetic approach to a complex system is done without the necessary analytical consideration of the component characteristics. Even if the dialectic materialists deny having omitted this important parameter in their design philosophy, it is obvious in Marxian socialism that its systems analysis deals mainly with the prediction of the results of interacting human components. If these results are satisfactory for the ultimate synthesis for a given goal, then the component characteristics are biased to fit the required vectors. At best, only those component parameters are utilized in the theoretical design which do not contradict the desired system dynamics.

Because the components of a social system are human beings, it is understandable that due to lack of information concerning all pertinent vectors which are relevant in social interaction of such highly complex independent units as men, many essential characteristics are overlooked or misinterpreted. It is also a tempting suspicion that the same high complexity is willfully misused by Soviet politicians to hide the flaws in their system, which can be detected only by careful examination by those few who are experts in the field. Therefore, it is psychologically understandable that the "facts" would be accepted by the human masses who do not possess the necessary information for critical evaluation, and must rely on the authority of the system's promoters. This trend is utilized and enhanced by clever emphasis of the hedonistic aspects of the proposed system or the threat of other systems against these basic human rights, as may be politically opportune.

The failure of the Marxian social system to integrate complex human individuality into their program resulted in the policy of the socialistic governments to de-emphasize individual (component) aspirations, unless they are directly promoting their system's goals. As a direct consequence of this policy, the materialistic dialecticians place their effort with respect to automation and intelligent machines on two areas: 1) enhanced production and 2) the conditioned assimilation of men to their machine partners.

The enhanced production of consumer goods is expected to increase human satisfaction and through it bring about the "gratitude" of the needy masses with the subsequent submission to the "advice" of "big brother." By the conditioned assimilation of men to their intelligent machine partners, the Soviet behavioral engineers expect that men will adapt and accept the uniformity of sophisticated automats and other devices of intelectronics, which is the science of artificial intelligence. As a consequence of such close adaptation, they anticipate that men will seek much less individualistic involvement. This, in turn, would simplify government by eliminating a certain number of the unmanageable dependent variables in the components of their social system. It is interesting, however, to note that, as the result of the continuous democratic bombardment of the intellectual Iron Curtain and the inevitable ideological hybridization of the socialistic countries with people from the democracies, the originally indoctrinated Communist philosophical ground rules are not any longer tenable.

This became dramatically manifest during the international conference "Peace on Earth." There, Marxist philosophers admitted the fact, and expressed their desire of closing the gap between the ideologies of East and West. Although the compliance with such a plan would mean for the democratic philosophy to make a few steps toward the left, these are mere ballet steps as compared with the strides which the Russian boots are seemingly willing to take. This break in the basically intransigent Soviet philosophy could be due to the realization that the cybernetic development of the human community will be a "forcing function" in the resulting trend of such hybridization. (The mathematical term of forcing function refers to an external variable which brings about a predetermined action in the system.) The present change in attitude in the Soviet policy can also be a clever political maneuver in the Sino-Russian relationship. This, however, cannot be judged exactly without having established intimacies with the Russian governing clique.

The picture is quite different, of course, if one analyzes objectively and entirely without gainful interest the possible effects of intelligent machines on the happiness of mankind.

First of all, let us dismiss the frequent, and somewhat desperate, question of materialistic dialecticians whether it is a prerequisite of desirable human existence to have "happiness." Everybody knows the ambiguity of the term "happiness." The information content of this word has different meaning for different people. It may range from a bowl of rice, through sexual satisfaction to spiritual fulfillment. It varies also within the same person, depending on such circumstances as the state of health and relative value judgment as compared with past experience, as well as in relating it to other people's similar feelings. To avoid lengthy, infertile discussion on this theme, let us be dogmatic (although we preach the opposite) and state, "Yes, it is a prerequisite." The existentialists may fight over this from their soap box, but we are contented with the recent trend of the mathematical approach to mental and emotional phenomena and its meaning in the so-called satisfaction functions.

Politics, in the best connotation of the term, deals with the human way of life in an attempt to optimize the circumstances which bring prosperity, contentment and happiness to all. Therefore, it is essential for politicians to be familiar with the changes which extensive automation will bring to human interest, desires and activities.

In a sketchy way, it should be demonstrated that the progress of cybernetics and the development of intelligent machines will enhance the *democratic* way of human interaction. The first symptom will be the drastic reduction of dependence of men upon the group, or "togetherness."

If the hardware of intelectronics and its peripheral automatic devices are designed into a humanoid shape, then this science is called robotics. Although such devices are still in the early developmental stage, they will become more and more sophisticated. In line with this, more and more material needs for which one man expects the physical service of another man will be done by intelligent machines or at least with the aid of them. Therefore, the economic servitude of the taxpayer will gradually disappear. The central organization, which by then can hardly be called "government," will have to do only engineering design tasks and linear programing, which is a mathematical method for the control of the flow of raw materials and the production and distribution of products and power.

People have an enormous variety of individual talents, desires, and inclinations. With the help of cybernetic pedagogy and through the laws of large numbers, they will provide, in the truest democratic tradition, the necessary manpower for those activities which the system requires, but which the individual person is free to choose. Yesterday this would have been an improbable statement, and admittedly it will remain such for quite some time to come; but, based on past experience, it may become reality sooner than anticipated.

Automation and cybernetic organization will emphasize the democratic principles for a world in which the individual can freely choose his way of life and pursue his happiness. The machine partner will not impose on man his more or less mechanistic character. On the contrary, the intelligent machine will free man from those restraints which he must accept today to satisfy the need of an imperfect society. Consequently, it will also remove the necessity of conformity and will enhance the development of individuality, even more where it seems to be buried in inferiority complexes.

It becomes obvious that the task and the method of politicians, in an era when human values and political promises can be quantified and digitalized, thus evaluated by computers, will be radically different from his present activities. Of course, much will be lost from the emotional excitement of elections, because any candidate can find out in advance his chances of being elected, if he interrogates the computer and compares his own values with that of other candidates in reference to the salient issues. It is beyond doubt that if the necessary technology is available, the people will, sooner or later, demand its utilization, because the computer assisted election will save the taxpayer millions of dollars and at the same time will increase the fidelity of his choice of candidates.

10.
THE ROLE OF CYBERNETICS
IN HUMAN HEALTH CARE

Space technology has shown the road and an example for information processing of data from a highly complex system for the purpose of human decision-making. This achievement became necessary to enable the astronauts to operate their system efficiently. Their function can be compared with that of a physician when he makes his decision of curative measures based on the information which he obtains from his observation and from tests and measurements. It is strange that when we have developed the instrumentation and modern techniques to keep and repair the health of the astronauts in space craft and on the moon, some persons should still use the methods of yesteryear in the medical laboratories and in the physicians' offices. It is important to speed up the transition and apply space technology spin-off and cybernetic methods to human health care.

The problem area and the goals are clearly defined:

1) Develop methods for fast, precise and inexpensive measurements to detect subclinical aberration in human health.
2) Develop norms and standards to compare the measurements with high fidelity and reproducibility.

3)   Reduce the diagnostic load of the physician.

4)   Reduce the cost of information acquisition from the human body through automation, with special reference to biochemical data.

5)   Establish significant and subset-specific correlations, as well as second and third order interactions between measurable parameters to increase the meaningfulness of the measurements for the individual patients.

6)   Increase manpower by using semi-skilled labor to obtain samples and raw data.

The main argument for biomedical mass measurements is the important need for the establishment of a yard-stick to which one can compare faulty operations of the human sub-systems. The process of obtaining the necessary information is called biomedical profiling or multiphasic screening. Some of the practical requirements are:

a.   the measurements should be significant for the local health environment and be specific for the local population,

b.   the retrieved information should tie into the already existing programs, e.g., malaria, tuberculosis, etc.,

c.   the measurements should be quantifiable, thus lending themselves to electronic data processing,

d.   the necessary instrumentation or the obtained samples should be mobile or semi-mobile, and

e.   the cost-effectiveness of the measurements per parameter and individual should be high.

Biomedical profiling is experiencing great interest in all phases of health care. Therefore, it is necessary to look at the cybernetic system of bioanthropological characteristics of given segments of population, and try to discover the major parameters necessary for the maintenance of well-being of various population groups. The origin of the factors which cause performance decrease in man can be intrinsic, extrinsic or both. Although most people involved in providing health care are dealing primarily with the human being himself, the cybernetic approach to health requires that all, even second and third order interactions, should be taken into consideration. Consequently, the very significant influence of the outside environment cannot be omitted in such a study.

Most students of this field feel that the total scope of human health is so complex that an approach to a general model is quite hopeless. In first approximation this may seem to be so, especially for a cardiologist or a biochemist. However, a biocybernetician, or a cybernetician in general, is accustomed to dealing with large and ultra-large systems, where the component density and subsequent systems output are far beyond the comprehension of a human mind. Fortunately, the methods of cybernetics and the development of intelligence amplifiers* point the way toward possible solutions of a problem syndrome of the magnitude of general human health.

Tons of gold and millions of man-hours have been spent in the study of health. Most of it has been directed toward the supreme goal of curing the sick. Some has been used to detect the reasons for the pathological state. And a little has been used to establish preventive steps. But the comparative effort to get good, valid measures, baselines and tolerance limits for the various standards is insignificant and the systems analytic approach is, comparatively speaking, almost nil.

Of course, human health cannot be viewed as a general system, because it is a large set of diversified sub-systems, which are more or less stabilized in a spatio-temporal coordinate system. Each of the sub-systems has its dependent and independent variables, and what makes it totally inaccessible for the information handling capability of the human intellect is that even the constants are in continuous, dynamic and highly non-linear change in the time domain.

The knowledge of the interaction of biological, psychological and environmental factors is not new. Yet most measurements are nothing but raw data of a single parameter; or, at best, a very few interdependencies are taken into consideration. But even these are so coarse that in many cases they become somewhat meaningless. Thus, many quantitative or semi-quantitative system read-outs have a very low fidelity. Such factors which are irrelevant without many correlated parameters are, for instance, age and sex. Also, the sample space is frequently poorly defined, as in the case of profiling, for example, a few hundred physicians. This has meaning only if the goal is the detection of possible professional detriments, or prevalent characteristics of those who have chosen medicine as a profession. Furthermore, by scanning the literature of biomedical profiling, one does not find the so-called Central Limit Theorem* applied to the statistical evaluation of biomedical raw data. Yet it seems that it would be most useful in dealing with data from a population with multiple heterogeneity. But this is a systems, or rather cybernetic, approach to biomedical profiling, so I shall leave the fascinating story of statistics to the statisticians. I am fascinated by statistics because in a certain way it is kin to cybernetics: it is a *human intelligence amplifier.* The mass of raw data coming from systematic measurements of given parameters are mostly meaningless rows and columns of figures to the human mind. Only intensive and time consuming study reveals inherent structural characteristics of the information. However, the proper statistical techniques will process that information and present it to the human mind in a form which is readily accessible to the brain for cognitive and decision-making purposes by keeping the dynamic flow of information within about 50 bits per second, which is the average brain capability. The raw data, of course, may contain millions of times more information which do not contribute significantly to the conceptualization of the inherent regularities of the assembled measurements.

A new dimension opens up for biomedical profiling by using cybernetic and bionic techniques. The usual method in obtaining statistical data is to select a certain parameter which is hoped to be of significance in judging and comparing biomedical data from a certain population segment. The next step in the usual profiling is to establish the physical and chemical messages which one can obtain from the individuals with good reliability and by measurement. The third step is the establishment of analytical processes with which the information samples can be quantified; and, finally, there is the mathematical manipulation of the obtained data for the purpose of extracting certain laws or regularities which can be used to recognize biological characteristics and establish reference points to detect pathological deviations.

In order to provide examples, let us look first at the

cybernetically controlled system of human blood.

Blood contains components which represent the various variables in this biological servo-system which is, under normal conditions, in homeo-dynamic steady-state. The various organs and other sub-systems in the human body react on, and influence, the composition of the blood by varying the distribution of the components.

It is obvious that by taking a blood sample and measuring the static concentration of a given component in it, we are examining only the system's output. Yet the purpose of these measurements is to obtain a diagnostic value with which we can determine the malfunction of the components of the system. The more individual static concentrations are measured and correlated with each other the closer we get to the understanding of the functional integrity of the components in the "black box."* The understanding of the regulatory mechanism of such a complex system as is the blood can be approached only cybernetically. This means that one must construct a model which is capable of reproducing a self-regulated system able to choose and determine the goal of its activity and capable of establishing its program characteristics and also alter it according to circumstances. Most physiological regulatory systems are of this "epigenetic"* nature.

Another important and most remarkable biocybernetic regulatory system in the human body is that of *glycemia.* Essentially this system acts on the *glycogen* reserve with two antagonistic sub-systems, namely, the *hyper-* and the *hypoglycemic* systems. Hyperglycemia, namely, the message of too high sugar concentration in the blood, acts, on one hand, on the Langerhans-Islands in the *pancreas* by controlling *insulin* secretion; on the other hand, it influences the *hypothalamus* which also acts on the pancreas through the *pneumogastric.* The chemical messenger, *insulin,* inhibits the action of a *somatotropic hormone* in the anterior lobe of the *hypophysis.* As a consequence, the enzyme *hexokinase* can degrade glucose from glycogen and deliver it into the blood stream. Both of the aforementioned feedback loops result in the decrease of the blood sugar level. Very typically to all, even mechanical automatic control systems, such oscillating control activity over-shoots somewhat and reduces or increases the sugar concentration in the blood below or above normal level. We are dealing here with a very typical cybernetic mechanism called "regulation by means of error." Small errors will pass through the control system; and that constitutes information which is transferred to the regulators to make them ready to inhibit the occurrence of *larger* deviations.

From the thousands of examples in biocybernetics these two relatively simple ones were chosen to illustrate the thesis that the fidelity of a therapeutic decision which is based on the type of measurements which biophysical and biochemical raw data furnish to the physicians must be relatively low because it is incomplete information. The main purpose of the physician is to recognize and correct the faulty component operation in the ultra-large system of the human organism. The efficiency of his operation depends on the analytic or diagnostic information which he can obtain. Unfortunately, the mind of the physician in his information processing capability is limited to a flux of information of about 50 bits per second. Consequently, if we confront the physician with a mass of raw data referring to relative values between the norm and that of the patient, and regardless of whether this information is displayed through all of his sensory modalities, including olfaction, kinesthetics, audio, as well as the visual display of charts, curves, and pictures, he can utilize all this information only at the rate of the incredibly small figure of about 50 bits per second for decision-making. With the presently available methods, we are providing so much information to the physician that he is, in most cases, in sensory overload. As a consequence, he can use for therapeutic decision-making only a very small fraction of the available information. The mind of the physician is utilizing "Gestalt-theoretical" factors to recognize shapes of curves or picture elements without time-consuming, cognitive activities. But this gives him only a small crutch to cope with the information explosion which he is experiencing. Yet, we are complaining that the present state-of-the-art of diagnostic methodology, especially in the provision of biochemical and biophysical data, is totally inadequate and primitive because it does not provide the physician with anything but integrated system or sub-system outputs, without the detailed component characteristics of the system in question. If the cybernetic approach to the diagnostic efforts in medicine would become a reality, then the amount of information available to the physician for his therapeutic decisions may increase by a factor of 100.

Now, let us make the already hopeless situation even worse by pointing to a new, but nevertheless most significant, problem area. This is an expression of the cybernetic nature of the sub-systems in organisms, namely, visceral learning. What that means is that as long as we have not developed a methodology by which we can distinguish whether, for instance, the elevated concentration of a given enzyme is brought about by functional diminution of a component of a diseased organ, as in the case of a *myocardial infarct* (in the heart) or whether the level of the enzyme production is due to some unknown fancy of that organ, we remain in a sad state of affairs as far as the pragmatic healing of people is concerned.

Who knows, maybe there is a new avenue of healing opening up in front of our eyes, where the physician's main tool will be education; where he will teach and train his patient to lower his blood-pressure or *cholesterol* level with an intrinsic autonomous mechanism, instead of symptomatically by drugs with inevitable side-effects. Whether it will work and supplement so-called classical methods remains to be seen. But we have to try radically new and more efficient avenues toward the betterment of mankind!

The work in the direction of general biomedical screening is making good headway. In the United States, Japan, Australia and elsewhere we are on the threshold of being able to assemble good and plenty of data from various population segments. These will greatly contribute to the understanding of the dynamic character and specific nature of the human body chemistry.

As a cybernetician, one would suggest that the next practical step in automatic diagnostic analysis should be the following:

Through intensive processing of available data and those accruing from multiphasic screening, the human subset variations should be quantified and the values deposited in the analytic automat. The patient's characteristics, which are gathered in any case, by admission to the hospitals, are punched into a card which is inserted into the automat. The print-out on the card will show only those values which are abnormal, ignoring normal parameters, but it takes into consideration all known base-line variations due to sex, age, race, pregnancy, etc. Such a technique will eliminate the possibility of overlooking a significant value on a crowded chart, which now occurs not infrequently and can be explained by a cybernetic approach to information displays. The physician's mind has to process data, if he sees them, whether unusual or not, but negentropy* value is only in the information from abnormal data. Then why burden his decision-making, cognitive functions with useless messages?

There is much opportunity to improve and advance the state-of-the-art in automated diagnostic analysis. It is advisable that biochemists, biophysicists, psychophysicists and the physicians should keep in close contact with system analysts and biocyberneticians to bridge the communication gap. This will make progress jump, not just crawl, as we have experienced it in the past decades.

Automation in this field must fulfill the following requirements:

1) automatic techniques should be as precise as the best manual methods;

2) automated analysis should be more economical than the manual, by taking capital outlay depreciation and maintenance of the automat into consideration;

3) automated technique should provide results faster than the manual ones;

4) automated analytical procedures should have a higher diagnostic potential than the conservative manual method;

5) automation should increase the professional opportunities of the personnel involved in diagnostic analysis;

6) automation should improve the patient-physician relationship;

7) automated analytical information retrieval should cause minimal inconvenience to the patient; and

8) automation of diagnostic data gathering should free the man-power involved in health care to enable them to care for a greater number of patients.

Turning these requirements into questions, all of them can be answered in the affirmative, beyond a shadow of a doubt. This clears the road for progress in this field. Countries, progressive or not, cannot afford to go any other way; especially those where health care is placed on the shoulders of the taxpayer.

11.

CYBERNETICS IN MARINE SCIENCES

*Glimpses of a field without
human interaction, where the
laws of the systems sciences
are manifest.*

The neural mechanism in intelligent organisms developed in the past into a self-organizing, self-optimizing cybernetic system. This system is distinctly divided into two sub-systems:

1.   One type of mechanism is developed to perceive stimuli from the exo-environment, which can operate either by direct contact: such as taste, temperature, or touch, or it can sense at a distance: by sight, sound, smell, etc.

2.   The second type deals primarily with data-processing and psychomotor functions. The stimuli of the endo-environment provide important collateral input information.

The input receptor accepts information in the form of stimuli from the environment and stores it in the memory. The memory can store information for a longer or a shorter time, depending upon a set of variables. Besides storage, the brain cells perform logical operations according to a preprogrammed pattern, and aim mostly at the solving of problems which are presented to them.

Furthermore, the brain cells provide the cybernetic task of synchronized control of mechanical operation of body structures, whereby the proprioceptive* sensitivity of the organism is of great assistance.

Turning now to the Marine Sciences, a cybernetic approach can be taken for better understanding of such behavioral problems as those encountered in the study of a school of fish. It can be shown that the probability of individual survival is greater in a school than if the fish is solitary. This is amazing because a superficial logic may indicate that the detectability of a school by a predator is much greater than of a single individual. Yet the probability of the survival of an unaggressive solitary fish in the environmental time-space dimension is much less than if it is the component of a large system of the school. The avoidance reaction of the group skews favorably the chance for survival of any given individual. This is partially due to the fact that if the predator has received enough bits of visual information on the desirability of the prey, it makes the pursuit decision and visually locks on that individual target. The pursuit task of the predator requires a high degree of vigilance to overcome the evolution-generated defense capability of the prey.

In the presence of a school which performs an avoidance maneuver, the predator receives so many visual cues which have a hedonistic value that it creates a significant noise in the psycho-motor function of the predator which, in turn, interferes with vigilance. This interference is due to the overloading of the predator's brain in its decision-making mechanism by a too high flux of information which is channeled to the center of his central nervous system by the sense organs. This interference is the increased chance for the individual in the school. That the hungry predator will eat, due to this interference, another member of the school is of little concern to the fish in question.

Many solitary fish use programmed information developed by evolutionary selection to increase their survival chances by decreasing the signal/noise ratio in their visual environment. This is called "mimicry" in classical biology. The predators, in turn, refine their scanning capability and try to extract by various means useful information from the noisy environment. The feedback results in a food-chain homeostasis, which is commonly called the balance of Nature.

In spite of the fact that it has been discussed before let us mention again that cybernetics helped us in the definition of life. The best brains of mankind have struggled with this problem without having found an unobjectionable solution. With the aid of cybernetics it may be stated or defined that *any self-organizing, self-repairing, self-reproducing system which perceives stimuli from the environment and which can process and organize that information in a goal-directed way, is living.*

This definition has the advantage that it is applicable to extra-terrestrial life. Of course, one can also foresee that in some future time bionics and sophisticated automation may develop devices which will show all the above characteristics. Then the time will have come when the distinction "living" versus "non-living" must vanish from our nomenclature, *when we will have to admit that a device can be an organism.*

Another criterion for life is the ability to recognize material reality of the environment. This realization is brought about by sensory perception which can also be duplicated by artifacts. The nature of sensation and the perceptive organs are the subject of innumerable studies in biology and psychology. The original five sensations have been outnumbered and we are still detecting more and more means of organismic interaction with the environment. Sensory perception of wind-speed, the plane of polarized light, chemical compounds, the direction of infrared radiation, x-ray and gamma ray sensitivity, magnetic flux and others have been carefully investigated and man's perception to them explored. However, there are numerous others which are still puzzling. For instance, what kind of an interaction exists between the fisher bat and the fish? What kind of a signal does the bat receive when it flies low over water, then suddenly dips his claws under the surface and comes up with a fish every time? It is probably not sight. It is not smell.

We know that almost every species of fish has an electric receptor which is tuned to certain specific wave-length, wave-form, pulse duration and pulse code. With this "locator" the fish receives information about shape, size, etc., of objects in its neighborhood.

Some fish can locate permanent magnets or isolators placed outside of the aquarium.

The extensive electro-reception in fish is demonstrated by the electrical field which is generated by the membrane of the families of Gymnotidae, Mormyridae and Gymnarchidae. They emit relatively low-frequency impulses, of about one volt, continuously. This activity has, of course, an entirely different purpose from the electric discharges of certain eels and rays.

A challenging problem for cybernetics in the marine sciences is the so-far unsolved mystery of how the fish in the rear end of the school communicate and control the movement of the leading fish in a school. There is enough evidence to prove that the "leaders" are in the *end* of the school of fish, and the school becomes temporarily disorganized if they are removed.

Regarding the fact that marine biology is greatly interested in lower forms of life, uni-cellular organisms in particular, it seems appropriate to discuss here briefly the cybernetic aspects of the cell.

Due to the large number of chemical and physical events which establish the operation of the cells, it is quite difficult to construct a model for a generalized cell. All one can say is that it gives better insight into the cybernetic model conception if one revises the definition of the cell.

One can say that the operational integrity of a cell is based on a specific morphological structure and concomitant dynamic chemical and physical processes in an open system which is capable of information processing and subsequent regulatory activities. A disturbance in this system is called *disease* as long as the homeostatic mechanisms are able to reverse the disturbance to the original equilibrium, and is called *death* if the process is irreversible.

The difficulty in the generalization of the definition of a cell arises from the fact that the term "cell" is applied to an RNA- or DNA-type virus, as well as to a complex protista, like the euglena, or a highly specialized cell like those which are producing a hormone, or as is a neuron.

If one analyzes the cybernetic interrelationship of cells in organs and in the organism *in toto* then it can be seen how the structurally, or rather, the cybernetically required functional and spatial unity of self-organization establishes shapes and sizes, which cannot be broken down into small autonomous systems, populations, niches and symbiotic entities such as certain marine bacteria, etc.

In the cell one can clearly detect, although with some conditionality, the flow of external and internal information. The exchange of molecules within the nucleus is definitely a code of a certain order and can be considered as internal information. But the cells exchange chemical messengers between themselves, even those which are, biochemically speaking, at a great distance from each other. For example, there is a cell which produces luciferine, another which generates luciferase. With the automatic or willful interaction of these two compounds, the fish can generate light. These end-products are synthesized in the inside of these cells, which read those codes at highest level. But the precursors of these compounds are probably manufactured in parallel cells and lower-coded sub-systems. The total light production in deep-sea fish, however, is a truly organismic activity in which the animal as a unit-system participates.

To exemplify this further, a human word, which is an auditory transmission of intelligence, is produced directly by certain muscular contractions in the neck and head. Yet they are the product of the total organism because the mental processes, which originate the psychomotor function of vocalization, are the result of the total endogenous system dynamics.

It is a fascinating field to study the cybernetic organization of marine protista. Of course, one can over-simplify it by saying that the entire activity of the cell is a read-out* of the program deposited in the DNA.

This, however, does not illuminate the complex system of feedback which gives the cell its flexibility and the ability of self-regulation. The informational DNA, for instance, acts as a messenger for transmitting information from the nucleus to the ribosomes,* thus activating the protein synthesizing mechanism of the RNA. Some of the RNA compounds are inhibitors which inform the nucleus about the state of the control function in the periphery, brought about by the newly synthesized compounds. Consequently, they will act as a sensor and switching system, which will turn on and off the synthesis factory for a given enzyme.

It seems that this process is not an "all or none" type activity, but it is a dynamic control whereby it can be assumed that the speed of the production of a protein can be slowed down or speeded up. The physico-chemical explanation of this phenomenon is thinkable only if one assumes that the messenger is a truly cybernetic entity and perceives information from the environment, processes this information by coding it in forms of energetics and also controls the process of synthesis. It may do this by increasing or decreasing the entropy of the process of synthesis, maybe by heating up or cooling down the synthetically significant part of the RNA molecule. This, of course, is strictly speculation. The truth we shall know only if the total process of the cybernetic operation of a uni-cellular organism can be modeled. We can only hope that the modeling of biological processes will one day be so sophisticated that all interactions within a cell will be understood.

Today, a question such as "Does a copepod* have consciousness?" is so remote from our scientific experience milieu that the seriousness of such question may be in doubt by some.

Yet, if one examines the cybernetic definitions of "consciousness" or "thought," they can be applied equally to man or uni-cellular organisms.

There is, of course, no way to expand these definitions at this occasion, but it may suffice to point out as a mosaic of this problem that if an amoeba proteus or a ciliate performs an "avoidance reaction," it reacts to environmental stimuli with the program to defend itself. Thus it must have some sort of concept of "itself" if it selectively "defends" itself against one stimulus but not against others which cannot constitute a threat. Hereby we do not refer to such passive defenses as a barrier against bacteria, a semipermeable membrane to "defend" the water or mineral household of the protoplasms, the buffers to maintain the optimal pH in the cell-sap against a "hostile" environment, etc. We had in mind only active defense, which is related to motion. It could be conditioned or unconditioned reflex in the broad sense of the word, or it may be willful activity based on "vigilance." This brings us again to metazoic entities, but if this term is defined from the aspects of information theories, it fits also the protozoa.

It is understandable that in the case of a complex organism, such as a fish, the various programs resulting in vigilance, or attention, will stimulate one set of components and inhibit others. In this competition very large numbers of various cells are involved. But it is most astonishing that such activity can be brought about within a single cell.

The cybernetic approach to fish behavior can be considered as systems analysis in marine biology. For instance, it is known that mackerel schools are observed mainly in the 50° to 54°F isotherm band in the water, yet such isolated empirical data may yield more valuable information if the total system is explored in its seemingly unrelated interactions.

Innumerable applications of cybernetics can be made to almost every aspect of oceanography, such as circulation pattern of the continental shelf and slope, fog formation, meteorological influences, etc.

Looking at the cybernetic aspects of systems analysis as it refers to the marine sciences, one of the most prevalent phenomena appears to be the elasticity of homeostatic sub-systems. A self-organizing system is called stable if most of its distinctive variables remain within given limits.

The system, to be able to maintain its equilibrium within the phase space, must receive a continuous flux of information from the environment. The system uses the energy represented by the negentropy of the information flux to counteract the energy gradient required by the second law of thermodynamics. Such information arrives to the homeostatic system as disturbance which, in turn, is channeled through a hypothetical "regulator" to the corresponding variables.

It has been shown that biological systems, which include not just a copepod, or a school of fish, but colonies, or even human societies, have the tendency to accumulate and store reserves in information. Mathematically this can be expressed with a so-called utility matrix which is used in decision theories. This activity somehow points to a parameter of such systems which resembles a primitive self-awareness, which one could call "group consciousness."

It has been shown that the homeostasis of the plankton*

community is significantly higher than the stability of the environment.

The fact that photosynthesizing and respiring planktonic organisms have been found in many hundreds of feet depth and on the ocean floor shows the complexity of living systems on one hand and the phenomenal inherent adaptability of life on the other hand.

It seems that, in spite of extensive research efforts, *we are still quite ignorant in understanding the true limits of terrestrial life.* Given enough time, under the stress of the environment and in the presence of proper mutagenic* catalysts, life forms can evolve with stable homeostasis which seem quite impossible if we use our present information inventory as a yardstick.

This thought gives some foothold for the anticipation of possible and probable forms of the anatomy and physiology of extra-terrestrial self-organizing systems.

12.

SOME CYBERNETIC ASPECTS OF THE
BEHAVIOR OF SOCIAL INSECTS

The new trend in bionics or cybernetics to analyze social configurations from the cybernetic point of view resulted in the creation of the sub-science called "cyberculture."

Cyberculture attempts, in essence, to define and identify various interacting channels and their information density with the subsequent feedback effects and the resulting control integrals of social gross behavior of man.

Due to the extreme spread of variations among humans, the development of an even approximate model for human social events is an almost incomprehensibly complex task and at this time an impossible undertaking.

If the systems approach of cyberculture could operate with more uniform components, the prognosis for success would be more favorable. This would only be feasible if the individual components would be much simpler than a human being. Therefore, it seemed prudent to start with far sub-human species; thus certain channel dimensions and signal characteristics would become more intelligible and would facilitate more sophisticated considerations for the human society.

A considerable amount of work has been done in research of the biophysical background of human social behavior, but only a few publications can be found dealing with the biophysical background of insect societies.

The pattern of the behavior of various social insects differs strongly. The approach to this complex problem was to choose a particular species for investigation. The caste of workers of the honeybee Apis mellifera was selected because there is a wealth of information available on its behavior. Yet little is known as to whether the duties performed by worker bees are voluntarily chosen or forced upon them by a motivation or an induced thought pattern. It can also be that the duties are assigned to them by some hierarchy, in the form of a control function and as a consequence of specific information. What can be observed is that, in a hive, cooperation and coordination are carried far beyond the mere solitary activities of individuals which are in the same developmental or physiological state, and in the same niche.

If we assume that the activity of a bee is a self-imposed task, the desire for such activity might be controlled by some physiological stimuli. It is impossible that the newly emerged worker bee is exclusively occupied in feeding the larvae because that is one of the least energy-consuming activities in the hive, provided we disregard the temporarily acquired job of attending the queen. It is also possible that the worker bee assumes its various responsibilities because it has learned them either by imitation or by being taught by older members of the society. The concept of "instinct," which is a working-form which we are using to describe a phenomenon and to substitute for our ignorance of the mechanism, should be disregarded here.

Most young bees do the same work in spite of numerous other possible activities, which are not dependent on any physiological prerequisites. A good example is dehydrating honey or fanning air into the hive. Yet the initiative factor in such an over-crowded and very complex society as the hive can be of little significance. Also, some probably learned activity such as building cells would be carried out mechanically only until a more dominant stimulus, such as hunger or fatigue, interferes with the activity. In the case of feeding the larvae, the picture becomes even more complex if we bear in mind that different types of larvae receive different diets. A certain larvae will get food where the protein-carbohydrate ratio is changed from day to day according to a precise scheme which determines the developmental outcome of the emerging adults.

The assumption of a particular job might also be the result of an exclusion principle. This means that, if most of the other activities are filled, the feeding of the larvae may be the easiest work whereby an abundance of food is assured the individual. Through this exclusion principle, the inexperienced young bee is directed into the least strenuous occupation.

The young worker bee will, however, not indulge in the assumed activity for an indefinite time. With the advancement of the life cycle of the community, other activities become available which then may be filled by random choice or by some unknown determining factor. Since the number of emerging young bees is small, as compared with the number of vacancies in a growing colony, it seems possible that every young worker bee should easily find an opportunity to choose the feeding of larvae as her occupation for a few days.

It is not known whether this is a hierarchy or some sort of "peck-order" among the worker bees, as can be found among some termites. It also seems improbable that feeding the larvae should be a submissive occupation; otherwise, some aggression would be notable and it could be expected that some of the young bees would assume various other occupations. Neither of these responses, however, has ever been observed.

The cleaning of the cell bottom and removal of the remains of the capping are carried out by bees 7 to 21 days old. Cleaning of the cell walls is done only by 1- to 12-day old bees and smoothing the edges of the cells by all ages, but mostly 1- to 6-day old bees.

Further interesting facts in the behavior of bees, related to feeding habits, can be observed through the administration of honey containing a radioactive tracer. An attempt in this direction has already been made.

Besides the feeding of larvae by young bees, there are, of course, many other activities of the members of a hive. They are difficult, if not impossible to explain without the assumption of a neuron chain-reaction which bridges over from a primary sensory excitation to complex neuron ring-circuits resulting in "free will."

It would be interesting to gather facts on the interdependence and personal freedom of individuals of a bee society and to try to apply the mathematical expressions to them which were developed for men. For instance, certain logarithmic satisfaction functions can be tried, such as developed by Rashevsky* which contain values for the measure of altruistic behavior. But, of course, we must use a special operator* which will account for the specific neuron configuration of bees. The mathematical deductions of the cooperation of social groups developed for a human social configuration can have aspects which may be made congruent with patterns of a bee hive.

Other features in group actions of social insects, however, have to be dealt with in a somewhat different manner. The asymptotic part of the curve of a human logarithmic satisfaction function, which can be the picture of prodigality,* does not coincide at a first approximation with that which can be seen with insects. Among bees and ants, the distribution of desire in function of the availability of energy libido* seems to be strongly positively skewed, if we take the human pattern as the normal curve. It is unlikely that any comparative research concerning occupational distribution would demonstrate great similarities with human society in which the individual freedom to choose a certain occupation is related to, and inversely proportional with, the population density, and which is one of the important vectors in the cybernetic machine of a beehive.

In a human society, the availability of resources and the relatively inefficient, or rather inelastic, industry offer commodities which fall short of the need to satisfy a variable number of individuals in an increasing population. In the case of honey bees, their society is admirably elastic. Within their normal life cycle, set by climate, seasons, and availability of food, there is almost no limiting factor for the growth of population, as far as the distribution of occupations is concerned. Of course, this takes for granted an abundant carbohydrate and proteinaceous food supply. The lack of a homeostatic equilibrium shows one of the open biological systems which becomes self-organizing as soon as environmental stress, like the lack of food, becomes manifest. It would be interesting to explore the communication dynamics of such an event.

Many zoologists and entomologists feel that it is highly improbable that an insect "knows" what it is doing. All actions are called "instinctive," that is, not learned but brought about automatically at the appropriate time. This hypothesis expressed in such general terms seems to be meaningless and of little practical value.

Most instinctive actions can be considered as an inherited motivation governed by a specific desire scheme, and brought about by complex stimuli on neurons. Unless we can find these proper physiological stimuli, we cannot accept as the driving force for certain actions of the bee an inherited, innate reactivity called instinct, because "instinctive" actions are due to semiconscious or rather subconscious perception of stimuli which happen to be resonant with the specific neurobiological structure of the individual. But there must be stimuli and special sense organs to perceive the stimuli. It is hard to believe that, for instance, young bees are stimulated to the elaborate feeding action merely by the sight of larvae. On the other hand, it is thinkable that for the production of invertase* or for the proper function of the pharyngeal gland,* the young adults obtain some kind of hormone from the larvae. Such a physiological symbiosis might easily account for a single or a multitude of information fluxes depending on the specific action of the biocatalyst.* The last mentioned possibility has already been investigated and found not to be the case.

So far so good, but how could one account for activities such as ventilation, dehydration of the honey, and guarding the hive entrance? Are these action-directed goals? If so, it indicates operationalism, that is, a behavior where action and thought are inseparable. Since the instinct is just a trigger, the desired action must be willfully pursued and organized. Consequently, it is rather probable that even insects would have a primitive logic with a typical pattern. If so, it is in some way qualitatively and quantitatively, but probably not essentially, different from a human thought.

Our limitation in obtaining information concerning the possibility of insect thoughts is due to lack of means of communication. The very effective stimulus and its reaction which has been most frequently used in communication with animals is that of appetite. Most of the training experiments are based on reactions to food gathering. What would be the reaction of a bee society to an artificial bee model which by some means could be moved about in the hive and which, for example, would imitate a dance indicating a rich nectar source? If the model is good and satisfies the visual and maybe olfactory senses of the bees, could it fool them and make them fly to a certain imaginary forage place? Or do the bees have a more complex communication system which involves some different type of receptors to which there is no parallel in higher animals or man? It has been proposed that certain insects possess a symbolic *emotional language.*

Bees, like other animals, orient themselves in general by taxis and kinesis. The first factor will cause the bee to move toward or away from a source of stimulus; the second factor will determine the speed and rate of turning induced by the stimulus. There are various persistent stimuli acting upon the bee, which it will pursue permanently until either an external bias cancels it or a stronger transversal information flow changes its vector.

It is established that a bee, having learned from a dancing worker the location of a rich food supply, will fly out non-stop to the indicated place, disregarding flowers on her way which she must have seen or smelled and which she probably would not have missed to visit if on a routine gathering trip.

This behavior indicates that the original stimulus is causing an amazingly long-lasting excitation and has an intensity which is not cancelled out by such primordial stimuli as sight and chemoreception.* Since in both cases the desired aim is food gathering, the blocking out of later stimuli can be explained by *willful choice, or an implanted subconscious control.*

It has been found that the time-perception in bees is brought about only by training and is independent of visual or metabolic stimuli, in contrast to ants, where it is dependent on metabolism. It is quite amazing if we consider that, with the relatively few axons in his brain, the bee can localize reference points in time and space. By the present status of our knowledge of the neural mechanism, it can be understood that with a perceptive stimulus, such as the plane of polarization of sunlight, a reference to a direction can be conveyed to the hive mates; furthermore, it can be accepted that there is a time memory in the nerve center of the bee, and that distances are indicated by flight times along the directional straight. The distance and direction are given by the dancing bee regardless of obstacles, such as a cliff or large building, and without accounting for turns and delays of the detour.

To mention another outstanding example of what appears to be rational thinking, there is the logical and highly deductive reasoning in the decision of a bee swarm to occupy a new home. It is well known how the information, brought in by individual scouts, obviously is weighed by a part of the total community and a final decision made. Only after all dancing bees are unanimous in the choice will the swarm depart. The means of communication must be very specific and complex because 30-40 bee scouts are flying in all directions and at distances ranging between 100 yards and 5,000 yards; all scouts cannot find the same cavity in a tree trunk in a forest with many equally good cavities. If we would assume that the routine dance and its resulting forage flight is some sort of a conditioned reflex in the worker's chemoreceptors and excited by the scent gland of the dancers, then why don't all the various scouts of the swarm have any followers in spite of the identical dance patterns? How can the colony choose, regardless of the number of the indicating scout group? Only *one* scout's "find" is followed by *all* the bees.

The approach to the problem can be attacked also from the point where a bee society gets in calamity. In such cases, e.g., if a bear is taking its dessert from a hive, the normal equilibrium is upset. The stimuli governing the routine tasks of the workers are still present: there are larvae to be nursed; there is honey to be dehydrated; there is the queen to be attended; and the drones fed. If the bees would be guided only by innate reactivity, those individuals which have nursed the larvae or have fanned the honey would be induced by new stimuli to do the repair work. But this is not the case. It has been observed that, in cases of disaster, individuals weigh the importance of the tasks and sometimes even neglect the offspring and the foraging. They leave their present work and start to collect or to secrete wax. It seems unlikely that strong stimuli, such as hunger and reproduction, could be cancelled out by the sight of a hole in the hive or some crushed cells.

On the other hand, if there is not enough food to satisfy all inmates, an increasing dissatisfaction must occur, which should lead to a forcible robbing of the supplies. This, however, never happens. The wax makers will be fed at a rate of 3 lb. honey for 1 lb. wax as long as the supply and some freshly gathered food lasts. Other bees would not increase their satisfaction by giving less honey to the wax makers. That may be due to a much higher tolerance threshold than can be found by many animals, or to other unknown psychobiological parameters.

All this points to a willful adaptation of an activity which can be considered as "motivational." This zoopsyche or animal intelligence is manifest in many insects in their imitative and learning ability. The habituation, and especially the formation of a choice in a trial or error type of experiment, supports this theory.

There must be some sort of distinction in bees for attractive and repellent sights even in cases where no primordial stimuli, such as resemblance to flowers, can be made responsible. For instance, bees will be attracted much more by the pattern X than by O.

It can be assumed that to a great extent, if not totally, the behavior of social insects is hedonistic. In other words, their activities are not forced upon them against their will by any other member of the society; rather, the individual adopts an activity because it increases its satisfaction. Furthermore, if a bee is able to get involved in an activity which has the same hedonistic value as one or more other possible activities, which do not have hormonal or other physiological prerequisites, the bee is making a choice. Again, to make a choice requires rational thinking in the Kantian sense, unless it is a random choice. A random choice and its statistical expression, however, would cause an entirely different behavior in insect societies.

It is evidently very difficult to accept rational thinking in insects. This is particularly true if we assume that an insect is or can be altruistic only to the degree where its altruistic action is directly or just slightly indirectly related to its own hedonistic pattern. To deny this would mean to expect in an insect such a complex emotional syndrome as is virtue. And this would be much more difficult to accept.

Hedonistic behavior, on the other hand, is brought about by two factors which can be expected in insects as well as in men. One is the genus-specific and inherited neuron configuration in the nervous mechanism; the other is the learned ability to select additive factors for one's time-pleasure continua. This latter ability is acquired by trial and error.

It can be argued that the worker bee's manifold activities are a reward for services rendered to the society. If an effective and complex way of communication among the inmates of the hive is excluded, such behavior must be based on experience. But is there enough time for a young bee to acquire such experience, since she starts her specific activity within a very short time after emerging? The species Apis mellifera is now millions of years older than Homo Sapiens. Could it be that she has evolved a neurophysical mechanism which is different from that of man? Nobody has thoroughly investigated this question, because physiological factors, such as the amount of cholinesterase* in nerve synapses, the similarity of neural transmission, or the action potential do not exhaust the problem. The answer to this question seems to be "no." This statement is based, however, on the shaky deduction that, according to the findings on the giant axon of the squid, this invertebrate's neural biochemistry and biophysics do not seem to differ essentially from those of men. Why should the bee be different?

Considering the interesting abilities of honeybees, it is amazing to see their illogical and maladjusted behavior in other situations, such as the lack of self-protection against the wasp Philanthus. The body weight of both insects is similar, and the success of the Philanthus is not accidental. Nobody has ever seen or heard of a case where the bee has subdued the wasp. Yet in experiments one can paralyze and eventually kill a Philanthus by injecting bee venom into its thoracic cavity. It has to be assumed that the bee-killing skill of this wasp has not been acquired by preying on other insects, since their anatomy might differ radically from that of bees. Consequently, the bee had the same amount of time to evolve a defense as had the wasp to develop its behavior. Or else the wasp is more intelligent than the bee, or the honey bee in her present evolutionary stage is a spontaneous mutant, having lost the know-how against this ancient predator.

It was intended by the author to throw a few spotlights on some phases of this interesting field in which he is doing research. Furthermore, it is hoped that these notes will induce enough interest by some biocyberneticians to pursue the problems of control and communication in a beehive and to carry investigations of the phenomena of social insect behavior beyond the state of a narrative description of observations.

13.
SOME CYBERNETIC ASPECTS
OF INTER-PERSONALITY INTERACTION

It has been long established that in the administration of test batteries for the establishment of personality profiles, especially by the type of tests as for instance, IQ, Rorschach, etc., the testor's personality has a distinct influence on the performance and results of the testee. This circumstance reduces, of course, the repeatability and with it the reliability of the test results.

The validity of a test can be demonstrated statistically with the aid of large numbers. Yet the same argument can be used to question the reliability of a test if it is applied to a single, special individual, whereby the analytical results of statistical averages are used as a standard.

It is well for the testor to try to conform with Freud's requirements of being completely passive in his testing behavior, but communication before and during the test cannot be avoided. And if there is communication between two persons, then, according to cybernetics, more information is transmitted to the testee than the number of bits which quantify the information content of the letter-group-symbols, called words, or pictures which are the test objects. There are virtual information entities, in gesture, facial expressions, etc., sometimes with enormous bit-values,* which will have significant effects on the testee's decision-making.

Latent or virtual information is greatly enhanced by the physical presence of the testor in the testee's environment. We have to assume that the testor is very experienced in the particular test; thus, during the test, as he registers the test data, he will early recognize certain patterns and partially evaluate the testee's personality. This feedback will invariably influence his empathy or antipathy which, in turn, will reflect back to the testee.

It was felt that this cybernetic system, which has similarities with the well explored man-man-machine complex, can and should be studied with the application of communication theories. Therefore, two tasks have been designed:

a)   the cybernetic mechanism of the inter-personality communication pattern; and

b)   a possible mathematical model of the interpersonality interaction.

It is obvious that if we are looking into the cybernetic aspects of the interaction between two individuals, we must first establish a distinct frame of interaction. Such restriction is necessary because of the large number of essentially different interactions which exist between two communicating persons.

There is no doubt that the interaction will rest on two main pylons, namely, the willful, predetermined transmission of verbalized physical or emotional information and the involuntary concomitant information which is mainly emotional in nature and becomes overt through transfer function via the parasympaticus* nervous system.

The channel capacity and the available energy, which are so essential in communication theory, are of little significance in our model. The reason is that the information flux in the type of system of our discussion is relatively small both in the visual as well as in the auditory sense modalities. Furthermore, much of the information is on a subliminal level, or by inference.

Another factor is that during pre-test communication both testor and testee may listen to each other's speech selectively which may bias *a priori* the attitude of the parties involved. The same goes, of course, for visual impressions. Although many overt behavioral expressions are inhibited by a testor who is trained to be passive, information is transmitted by mainly subconsciously governed behavior as posture, facial expressions, frequency of looking at the testee or avoiding his eyes, etc. Much depends also on the apperception of such weak signals on the state of vigilance of the testee. No doubt, an uninterested, apathetic, tired testee will be less receptive to such signals and will also offer less feedback to them.

First, the mechanism of the interaction between the two persons has to be studied by analyzing single events, rather than the dynamic system of all individual feedback processes. Besides the cognitive realization of visual and auditory cues, the human interaction is based to a significant degree on inference. Such inference is used by the testor and testee to make conscious or subconscious judgment about the nature, quantity and value of signals from the other person or persons present.

A theoretical approach to inference is based to a great degree on Brunswik's theory of probabilistic functionalism.† This describes how organisms arrive at inferential judgment concerning the characteristics of objects or subjects within their physical environment. In general terms, probabilistic functionalism is an explanation of cognition. In an extended form we utilize this theory to provide information on the operational mechanism when persons (or other organisms) are operating in a complex environment in which signals and static cues are utilized by inference to relay meaningfully characteristics of another person or object which is unknown to the person in question. The theoretical approach to this cognitive process is further complicated by the fact that the attributed characteristics are very unreliable as far as their repeatability is concerned.

Man uses inferential cues quite successfully by learning the probability of cue-values. Correlation analysis of inferential behavior could demonstrate the fact that man is using unreliable cues in various combinations and will come up with quite reliable inferences. It is well known in the cybernetics of electronic

---

†Brunswik, E. *Perception and Representative Design of Experiments,* University of California Press, 1956.

circuitry design and also mathematical considerations that one can arrive at reliable automata or other systems by using unreliable components.

In the case of a dynamic man-man-object feedback system, it is irrelevant, at least from our present objective point of view, whether the interaction is reliable or not, as long as any interaction is demonstrated.

From the hedonistic point of view, however, in the Szondi test* for instance, it is most pertinent which of the cards are attractive and which are repelling. Decisions on the part of the testee, which are skewed, due to the influence brought about by conscious or subconscious cues, are quite significant. Unfortunately, such bias cannot be eliminated by repeating the test six times or ten times, because the cue probability and their inferential interpretation will not just prevail as long as the same testor-testee system exists, but will be enhanced by the repetition of the interaction.

The investigations in this field yield an interesting experimental result which may be of some significance, namely, that it can be predicted that those cards which are hedonistically repelling are more easily memorized than those which are attractive.

It is unfortunate that at this time we cannot go deeper into the interesting analysis of the cognitive space and its hierarchy levels or dimensions with respect to the concomitant decision-making of the testee under the environmental stress of the inter-personality interaction. However, one would expect that a cybernetic approach and properly designed experiments would reveal results which can be used to improve the analytical as well as predictive value of psychological tests like the Szondi test.

We have to say, of course, something about self-optimization in this system, because it is an essential parameter of cybernetics. Self-optimization is really self-organization with a special state of equilibrium which is predetermined by a certain vector. Without this vector or forcing function the system would go into a different equilibrium. When we deal with humans, such a preferential equilibrium can also be called adaptive-purposeful behavior.

The system in the model of the Szondi test, for instance,

namely, testor-testee-cards, is seeking an equilibrium which it achieves by stabilizing all internal and external environmental factors in order to make the information flux from the card to testee as noise-free as possible. The interaction between testor and testee, although it represents noise, is of a character which skews the individual dynamic pattern of the system while it is in the process of reaching equilibrium, and cannot be considered as negative feedback.

The system, as it is manifest in the 48 cards of the Szondi-test, for example, is most complex by itself, but it can be expressed by simple set-nomenclature.* However, the system becomes even more complex if one analyzes the factors which influence the information flux from the cards to the testee. In the scanning of the cards by the testee, from the visual impression to the selection of the preferred ones, a large number of factors are playing a role. Many of these factors may be insignificant, but so far there is little known about their values. The process in itself is not very complicated: Visual impression—Meaningfulness—Value assessment—Decision—Action. But the number of the factors make the process almost hopelessly complex for cognitive comprehension.

Let us now approach briefly the aspect of the interaction between testor and testee. In establishing the probabilistic validity of psychological tests, like the Szondi test, the factor of the influence of the testor was an essential part of the testing environment. Otherwise, the presentation of the cards could be made easily automatic, or the testee could present them to himself.

Although the stability of these factors—namely, the inter-action vectors between the two persons—is not at all satisfactory, the end results are within the limits of usefulness. If it is possible to comprehend this significant factor more precisely, then one can assume that the test will be refined and consequently its reliability increased.

Because there is a feedback both ways, between testor and testee, there is an oscillating interaction between the two persons. This being one of the environmental factors, it will have an influence on the choice of cards, because the choice is emotional-behavioristic, and so is the interaction between the two persons.

It is obvious that only a brief spotlight was thrown on the problem complex of the cybernetic approach to psychological tests, of the type of the Szondi test, and that many research avenues in this field are open for fruitful exploration.

A promising one is the study of the Szondi cards with a variable grid to explore the value of physiognomic elements and their relationship to the hedonistic experience of the testee. Hereby one could also receive insight into the quantitative information content of the cards.

This chapter is intended to signify the cybernetic system testor-testee-testcard as a self-organizing system which is based on fluxes of information of various types with a resultant control function.

14.
A CYBERNETIC APPROACH TO THE EVALUATION OF RESEARCH PROPOSALS

Government agencies, universities and larger companies that are involved in R & D work and operate with a predetermined fund-structure are almost always allocating funds to individual proposals or projects.

The evaluation of the proposals is considered as a typical human operation, and the strongly subjective results, with all the human errors, were not overcome by farming out the proposals to more than one evaluator. Although this technique will increase somewhat the reliability of the decision, it is very expensive as far as time, effort and expense are concerned.

It is probable that a cybernetic approach to this problem may yield a system which can share and improve the human task to evaluation and subsequent decision-making.

The purpose of this chapter is to describe a semi-automatic system or device with which one can evaluate a number of research proposals with greater objectivity than by human decision alone. It is, of course, anticipated that the data will be processed before they are fed into the system. For instance, certain parameters of the presented material are put manually into categories and are quantified to provide numerical values which will be accepted by the system described below. If these values are not established by objective standards, then, due to the variability of the human, the fidelity of the system's read-out is diminished.

The evaluation of the proposals is performed in two steps, which represent the advancement and improvement over the present cumbersome and emotionally biased methods. Everybody knows that in spite of the best intentions of expert evaluators, unrelated factors, such as an upset stomach or an unappealing format of the description, will influence the decision. Thus, it could happen that such intangibles may influence progress; or, due to such bias, a less meritorious proposal is funded. The two operational steps which the projected system performs are:

1.   Establishment of the negentropy or the weighted probability of success of each research proposal.
2.   The establishment of the priorities for each individual proposal and an automatic distribution of the available funds.

The task which the proposed equipment should fulfill is related to the following problems and requirements: The proposals should be viewed as objectively as possible, with the elimination of most of the subjective human biases and errors. The proposals should also be evaluated a) when the sum total of the requested funds is greater than the available resources; and b) if the sum total of the requested funds cannot be programmed into the equipment because of the temporal distribution of the submitted proposals.

The proposed system is predicated upon four assumptions:

(1)   Utilization of a general purpose digital computer (GPDC) to perform a number of sequential operations such as assignment of a measure of subjective merit, determination of uniqueness, relevance examination, calculation of objectiveness (objectification), measure of the rational control of the proposed research, and an evaluation of the formal research objectives.
(2)   Due to certain random variables or indeterminate measures assigned during the evaluation operations in (1), there is

a digital output (measure) from this procedure which is an expression of a random variable.

(3)   A probability model should be constructed which defines the sample space of all possible outcomes for the computer generated measure of (1).

(4)   Because of the necessity of statistical processing of these samples, and because of the expense and time required to perform such operations on a GPDC, it is desirable to compute in real time the statistical values of the merit on a special purpose analog computer (SPAC).

The random outputs from the GPDC are converted in a D/A converter* to analog signals of a form which are acceptable as inputs to the SPAC. The analog signals are then processed by iterative integrating techniques* to produce the time-function of the estimates of the statistical mean x and variance RV of the function RV,x(t). By weighing these estimates, and by using an assumed probability model, an estimate of the probability P and its statistical variance are produced as analog outputs. These outputs are then available for storage and further computation by the GPDC following conversion in an A/D converter.*

Additional statistics may be required for the evaluation. If such is the case, the computations are readily possible with hardware additions to the SPAC. The negative entropy could be an output of either the SPAC or the GPDC.

In summary, what has been proposed is a hybrid computer form using a digital logic interface, a general purpose digital computer, and a special purpose analog computer. The GPDC is used for arithmetical calculations, data processing, memory, and decision—that is, those computational forms which it can best handle with accuracy and speed. The SPAC is used for statistical computations, integrations and real time simulation—computations which it can best handle with economy and speed. The "hands on" programming* capability of the SPAC also makes it best suited for modeling and effective use of the man-machine interaction. The digital logic interface is the control center for timing among these computers, the mode control of the SPAC, and program control of the GPDC.

In Figure 1 (see end of chapter) a flow diagram shows the processing of the individual proposals to arrive at a numerical negentropy value for each one of the proposals.

The equipment should provide the priorities among all received proposals, and should also give an instantaneous read-out for the amount of the funding of the project. Hereby, the total resources and other functions and variables established in the department of the funding agent will automatically be taken into consideration.

The proposed system should not only aid the fund administration in fair distribution of the available funds but should take into consideration peripheral information which, by exclusively human processing, would probably be neglected. Such negligence on the part of the evaluator is not willful, but is the result of the high information flux which overloads the decision-making capabilities of the evaluator. Thus, the information flux will be subconsciously, and according to the Gestalt theories, reduced to a comfortable operational level.

In Figure 1 the individual proposals enter into the problem processing. Here it is not just permissible but desirable that an experienced evaluator attach an arbitrary value of subjective merit or interest to the proposal. This factor represents the personal interest of the human component (evaluator) in the system. It must be expected that the person employed for this job is a scientist, who has experience in the specific subscience (bio-physics, medicine, chemistry, etc.) to which the proposals are restricted. His experience, knowledge and intuition should be used to eliminate those proposals which violate basic laws of nature, and to supply the complex integral value of a satisfaction function derived from his desire to promote the state-of-the-art. This is the only factor which is used at present in most cases in accepting or rejecting a research proposal. The purpose of this chapter is to indicate a way whereby the machine partner can help to close the gap between subjective merit and objective merit of a fund request.

The human component should furnish two values: a) the conformity with the basic laws of nature, which can have only + or - values. The "-" value must be well substantiated and should reject the proposal. The proponent of the proposal should have an opportunity for rebuttal of this point; b) personal interest should obtain an arbitrary value, such as one to ten. Then, the proposal will be processed according to the availability of similar research whereby the bibliography cited in the proposal cannot be considered a sufficient source of information. An arbitrary value should be established for the limits of similar research, also.

Too much research in the same field could be a demerit for the value. On the other hand, complete lack of available research in the same field may also be a diminutive value, because uniqueness of a research field requires extensive work at another phase of the data processing in this system. If the proposal does not fit into an arbitrarily set limit, it can be discarded at this point. The same thing holds for the next step, in which data are available in research on the same topic. After this, for practical reasons, the proposal is viewed concerning its relevance to, e.g., biophysics. Below a certain cut-off value, the proposal is automatically channelled to departments of other subsciences in order to utilize the proposal, although it may not fit into the requirements of the biophysics department. This, of course, is often a highly subjective decision.

After this process, this proposal enters the phase of objectification. Into this box is fed the objective assessment of whether the proposal conforms with the basic laws of Nature and is also compared with available research results from similar efforts. Then the proposal is subjectively evaluated to establish whether it has an unambiguous problem setting. Into this box is fed the information of administrative "Directives." From here the proposal is evaluated numerically concerning its creative-rational-adaptive control of the proposed research. Into this value are fed two vectors—the anticipated research result flux, which deals with a timetable of the research, and the quality of the research managerial decision plan.

The next step leads to the evaluation of the formal-factual-normative control of the proposed research procedure. Finally, the proposal should be graded concerning the optimal organization of the terminal objective.

All these values are fed into the computer complex as described above. The read-out of this device will provide a numerical value for the probability of success. The individual negentropy values of all proposals which were successful in acquiring a negentropy value are then processed.

The purpose of this chapter is to exemplify the practical usefulness of the cybernetic approach to such activities which did not seem to lend themselves to automation. It also shows that the human component can be well used in the communication and control functions as mediator for the achievement of the goal, where the state-of-the-art of the automat falls short in efficient problem solving.

FIGURE I

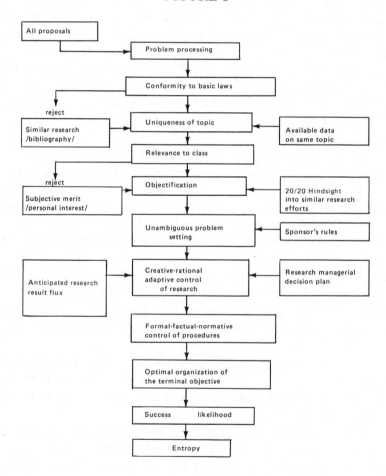

15.

AN APPROACH TO THE CYBERNETIC MODELING OF ONE ASPECT OF HUMAN BEHAVIOR

ENTREPRENEURSHIP

It is of considerable interest for our socio-economic system to find the parameters of the special attributes which enable a person to start and successfully operate a technical enterprise.

The entrepreneurial orientation of a large number of persons is the cornerstone of our democratic way of life. Furthermore, it is also of importance to modern management philosophy to employ entrepreneurs as leaders for technological sub-systems.

If we could establish through the analytical approach a model, or its approximation, of an entrepreneur, then one can generate a battery of tests which through a correlation analysis would yield a numerical probability for a testee's chance to become a successful entrepreneur. If such a quality is a prerequisite for a given job-profile, one could use such values in the choice of employment candidates. In approaching this problem, one finds that the parameters which should give a computable value for entrepreneurship can be used in a different assembly for many other aspects of human behavior. This is a spin-off from such research.

Intuitively, one assumes that for building a usable mathematical model for any aspect of human behavior one is confronted with an unmanageable number of parameters. However, regarding the fact that a first approximation to such a model would suffice as a point of departure, one can select a relatively small number of seemingly pertinent parameters and design the model with them. If such an attempt became successful, further sophistication can be applied to enhance the fidelity of the model. Also, the success of a technical enterprise rests only to a lesser degree on the entrepreneurial capabilities of the manager; a great deal rests on the social, economic and technological circumstances of the business operation. Therefore, it is sufficient to build a model which could give a *relative* probability of success of a person as compared with others.

To establish the useful parameters, one can subdivide the field either into genetic and environmental vectors or into the "background" and "foreground" of the individuals. One could, of course, apply known parameter inventories, such as Gattell's Sixteen Personality Factor Inventory,* or the Clyde Mood Scale,* etc., but more research must be done to find the most suitable set of data for a computer approach to solve this problem.

The interaction of genetic and environmental-temporal factors, as they establish a person's behavior, will always accrue information, and thus will increase the negentropy of the system. Therefore, entrepreneurship, as a preprogrammed set of dynamic organismic requirements, will have on its pathway a typical entropy distribution. If this is correct, then it is thinkable that one could advise a person in his attempt to enhance his chance for becoming a successful entrepreneur by manipulating those of his parameters which are willful variables.

In first approximation, an entrepreneur must have a set of genetic parameters which cause a typical and necessary behavioral profile. One of the outstanding requirements in an entrepreneur's hedonistic pattern must be the high value in his satisfaction functions for goal-directed problem solving. Another genetic characteristic of entrepreneurship is, among other things, the capability to optimize the value assessment of certain environmental data. Regarding the fact that "business," in the capitalistic sense, is related directly or sometimes indirectly to inter-personality interactions, called persuasion, the entrepreneur's task is to apply his derived values in his interaction with specifically chosen persons in the shortest possible time.

The time factor might turn out to be a critical factor in the model, because with the necessary genetic prerequisites and in a suitable environmental milieu everybody can become successful in business if the time-factor can be eliminated. However, in most of the cases time is of the essence, because of competition; and, what is even more important, the environment is dynamic. Thus, even if the entrepreneur recognizes the optimal condition for a transaction, he must act fast before the configuration changes. Furthermore, there is no question about the fact that the interaction of the specific parameters of genetics and environment, as they appear dynamically in the time function, are responsible for the overt behavioral attributes of entrepreneurs.

Before one can attempt to develop a mathematical representation of a biological system, or even a relatively small part thereof, a simple cybernetic chart of the known parameters has to be drawn, with all detectable interactions and feedbacks. Searching for the parameters of entrepreneurship one finds such complexity that the classical analytical approach becomes a *conditio sine qua non.*

With the aid of dimensional analysis, one can also attack the problem by constructing "analog" systems. The problem is to find the normalized quantities of parameters originating in the environment or in the genetic makeup of entrepreneurs. However, the difficulty in modeling human behavior, entrepreneurship specifically, lies essentially in two categories: 1) the large number of dependent and independent variables and 2) the non-linearity of the functions. The difficulty is further compounded by the great biological spread of the parameter data in human behavior, which, of course, is due to "intangible" variables. These variables, because of their nature, cannot be well quantified. Therefore, it is prudent to ignore them and to try to operate by regarding the illustration of such functions not as a line-curve, but as a band, or by applying the so-called parameter approach.

The "band" approach is very difficult to apply for a definite model because in these functions every point of the abscissa* has many ordinate values, thus the model will have indefinite characteristics. The same is the "parameter approach" which operates with sets and individual parameters which will appear in the model, although they cannot be written into equations.

In first approximation, two groups of factors are involved in the shaping of an entrepreneur: 1) genetic and 2) environmental.

In both of these areas there are many known independent variable parameters, but the nature of the functions is unknown. Possibly the Buckingham pi-theorem,* which deals with dimensionless responses of unknown forms to a set of known variables, could be applied to biological systems in a modified form. If this is feasible, then, in the case of human behavior, a dynamic similarity between the "mechanism" of the individual entrepreneurs could be established.

One could attack the problem of modeling the entrepreneur also from the point of view that by assembling information from his exo-environment for the construction of a business project, he is decreasing entropy. One can, of course, state in general that in a successful business venture a set of dynamic interactions takes place. This interaction between the entrepreneur and his opponent is a continuous feedback enhancement, which can, of course, have sometimes positive and sometimes negative values. In each of the entrepreneur's business activities in which he is directly confronted with a business opponent, such an interaction takes place. These interactions are quasi-sinusoidal.* The sine wave is dampened out as its curved base line approaches a maximum.

It is the typical skill of an entrepreneur to intuitively or willfully influence the amplitude, frequency and angle of these feedback oscillations.

In this chapter an intra-human, self-organizing behavioral system is sketched to show the complexity of the problem in its mathematical modeling, which is a prerequisite for bionic and robotic developments.

16.
CYBERNETICS OF HUMAN OPPORTUNITY

In the beginning, man was a hunting animal. He followed the wild herds and fished the streams and lakes; when he was hungry, he hunted, and when he made a kill, he ate. Soon he was right back where he started—hungry again. That particular feedback loop had no permanent gain. Even a moderate increase in his numbers placed a burden on the obtainable food supply, and kept him small and helpless. After a very long time, he recognized somehow, intuitively, the value of cybernetics and tried to use communications and control to improve his lot. He came to know the secrets of seed, planting, cultivation, and harvest. Then he could make an exponential increase in his food supply to match the exponential growth of his numbers in a new dynamic equilibrium. He settled down in the river valleys and there grew cities, empires, cultures and civilizations. It was this way until the Renaissance. Then man had a new experience with the exponential and with the feedback, and was confronted with the Scientific Method. The method of hypotheses and tests, which is essential here, can be looked at as a sort of a mechanism. He could make an exponential increase in the amount of useful knowledge, because he was unburdened by the information explosion as we know it today. In the earlier times, knowledge was related to the hunting process; progress was slow and handicapped by social disapproval, and often punished by those "leaders" who feared change. They are still with us, and are still a handicap to progress.

However, in the Renaissance, a loose servo-loop was developed where the hypothesis was used to test against nature. The error signal which came out of that test was fed back into the hypothesis, and when the error signal got below a certain level, a gate opened and the hypothesis was pumped into the knowledge bank. This was indeed essentially a servo mechanism,* and by it we are making today our exponential increase in useful knowledge.

Then came the emergence of the idea of progress, which in the agricultural societies was not reflected in man's philosophy. There the wheel of fate turned forever and got nowhere. In such a case, the only way to make a gain for a man was to impose a loss on other people. The idea of progress was absurd and up to two or three hundred years ago it didn't exist in any meaningful form. *It is a new concept.*

Out of the scientific method emerged a pragmatic, practical idea of progress—of making the world forever a better place for more men.

In all of history the scientific method, while it was working on the small volume of valid knowledge, produced, at first, a trickle of increase. This now is becoming a threatening torrent, which tends to get unmanageable in all its proportions.

The old "noise" of a static society, which came out of agriculture, was based on the assumption that nothing would ever change. This attitude, however, was often found to be inappropriate and invalid. Today we see, vaguely, the emergence of a new pattern. At first it seemed a new opportunity; later, a new threat. It can be both.

The present technocratic society is a combination of new powers with many of the old mores. It is beset by internal strains and internal inconsistencies; it cannot last.

What is coming is a new society based on the production and use of knowledge, rather than the production and use of food, with appropriate morals and appropriate men. The Russians, because they were early in social experimentation, have come early to the first attempt to produce this new kind of a "cybernetic" society. Their efforts began as a major state decision. Because it was early in the social revolution and because of its peculiar roots in Russia, with its peculiar ethnic, thus behavioral, patterns, it may turn out well; perhaps it will not. There is such a thing as trying to start something too early; maybe they did, and we see some regression toward the old scheme today. They have experimented with the complex problem of cybernetics. Their idea was to turn the whole of Russia, its earth, fields, seas, skies, machines, and men into one vast, planned, controlled and purposeful servo mechanism. Within this framework they have the concept of the Soviet man.

Produced by cybernetic processes of education and conditioning, they tried to develop a creature incapable of any thought against the will of his masters, burning with the desire to perform his part in carrying out that will—perfectly, flawlessly educated and conditioned, even to do creative research in this way. They wanted a super-efficient citizen designed to go with the future plan of Russia just as the future plans of Russia and its communications are at this moment being designed to fit him. Will they succeed? Who knows? They are making progress, and they are encountering problems. It is a tremendous research project to which the Russians have committed themselves. This, incidentally, is probably the real major threat that they pose to us, simply because we are not prepared to answer it. What do you do to a country that simply turns out to be relatively more efficient and more virtuous than you are?

Our situation is aggravated by our distaste for the use of the scientific method to develop the means to control human affairs. Anybody who attempts it runs into various kinds of social and political difficulties. This is a handicap which in the Russian state is the ultimate virtue. Who is going to make the fastest progress?

The problem, then, becomes one of preparing the United States, within the pattern and constraints of our present ideas about virtues and our present goals and our present morality, to meet and encounter this situation, and to win.

But somewhere and sometime in the world there will emerge a new dynamic society which will be based on the conversion of an ever-increasing body of knowledge into an ever-increasing power to deal with man and nature. It is probable that the human organism is capable of encompassing some of the old, yet of living with the new as he had encompassed the agricultural society in whose remains we still live.

Man is such an adaptive, self-organizing system that he can create an adaptive rather than a static society if he learns to apply the cybernetic approach. All it takes—what the Russians failed to achieve—is to design the human component in its present dynamic pattern into the system. The Russians had a good idea for an efficient cybernetic society, but they tried to force the homeo-kinetic* structure of the human component to fit their idea of society. All that has to be done is to design an optimized society based on the characteristic pattern of the available human component in spite of the great variability of the human resources. Of course, it is simpler to suppress or try to alter permanently the homeostasis of the individual components than to face the much more complex problem of a cybernetic design with highly unreliable and greatly diversified components. But the cybernetics of ultra-large systems, like the human society, happen to be very complex and difficult. The difficulty is further augmented by the fact that our knowledge of the human "black box" is very superficial. Thus, the component characteristics can be predicted only with low fidelity. But this does not have to stay so, and a concentrated effort could solve this problem. If this is so, essentially it makes no difference where the first beginnings of it occurred. The possessors of that culture will, however, run others away from the fair places on the earth and up into the hills, just as the agriculturalists did to the hunting tribes. You can find those hunting tribes still living in areas where their situation is beneath the average of their masters, and it is just not worthwhile to clean them out. Will we suffer the same fate, or will the United States manage to be the source of this new type of society?

The strategy of that new society is the use of change as a weapon and the use of progress as a weapon. The central feature of that strategy is not quite new. The USA embarked on it in the early days of World War II, and now we could not abandon it even if we wanted to. The scheme is to undertake to win by making worthless the investment of our opponent in mechanisms and in trading-in a trained man by imposing a change on our system.

Obviously, this works only if we are more change-worthy than the opponent. If our economics are not geared to continuous change and our education and orientation for change are not better than his, we better not embark on that boat. So far our performance has been, to put it candidly, marginal in this respect. We have not won. We might lose.

Ordinarily, when we looked back and saw the Russians catching up with us, we tried to run our research faster. Let's see what really happens in this model. In the first place, as time goes on, the ratio of the information available to the two contestants approaches one. This is a function of the diffusion-speed of information throughout the human community. This diffusion has two significant parameters of prime importance: communication and spying. Suppose that we start on a parameter with a ten-fold lead on our opponent's, and suppose that the intelligence half-life is about two years. This means that in two years half the lead will be gone and after a few half-lives, say ten, we approach the situation of defeat in this factor. This is based on the arbitrary supposition that our competitor did not do any research of his own; he only found and used ours. If we take into account the independent research of the opponent, it further complicates matters.

Now suppose that we accelerate our effort and hope that we are going to get back our lead. But, unfortunately, it seems to be gone forever. The other side will follow us in any such parameter with a lag which amounts to one half-life forever afterwards. When we accelerate our effort and intensify the contest in this way, it puts increased strain on our social and economic system and also on his with regard to the rate of change.

Let us assume that both countries have the same goal, namely, a technocratic development which utilizes natural resources and artifacts in an ever-increasing trend to provide a continuing improvement of their niche.

It is further assumed that due to the increase of both populations and limited natural resources, as well as an intangible philosophical value difference, each country considers the technological superiority of the other as a threat, which results in a technological competition. This is predicted in the Marxian philosophy.

The winner of such a contest obviously will be the one whose men and institutions are more durable and more efficient. It is not at all a matter of accelerating the research, unless our learned institutions are oriented to the contest.

Suppose, for instance, that the reader had a valuable new idea, a new design principle which, incorporated into the proper equipment and field, would make a great difference in our strategic posture. Suppose that it took two years for the Russians to find it out. Then they go to work on it. Their innovation time is often about five years; thus, in about seven years, the Russians would feel the power which is based on *our* information; and our soldiers and diplomats would sweat blood for three years on account of what *we* did. See what is meant? This is actually the predicament we are in now. We are doing the wrong thing because we are not sociologically ready and not enough system-oriented.

The *real* menace of the Cold War is not the party who is smart or fast with his research, but it is the side which is the master of change. This comes right down to the question, "How about the mastery of change?"

We must, then, use the factor which caused the problem; namely, the scientific method of research. Thus, we have to develop, for the first time in our history, a new society. Otherwise, we probably will be too late.

But how does one research and develop a dynamic society with an optimized system of interactions? There are a few factors which should be mentioned as possible parameters.

At first let us consider man, the dynamic, technologically oriented man. Today, in our present social structure, a man's profession disappears in about ten years, at which time he has to re-educate himself. During his working life he starts with the equivalent of four or five years' college courses to get into the lower echelons of professionalism. The importance of his position rises and falls kaleidoscopically as he watches the machines change, and the organizations which are in perpetual turmoil and transition. One can ask some famous anthropologists to help design a society. At first they will throw you out of their offices. After strong insistence they probably will tell you: "You don't research and develop a society. It takes a thousand years or ten thousand for one to grow, and we don't know how it does it."

You may convince them that maybe we don't know how, but that we have to do it. Then they will begin to talk, and you can learn some interesting things from them.

They will tell you about the concept that they call the "Social Myth." This myth, which is not anymore a myth, is the thing that the explorers found in the underdeveloped tribes as they began to study them. They heard about the things by which these men and women lived and died. They seemed ridiculous to them and they didn't believe them at all, so they called it the "myth." Gradually, the awareness of what the "myth" is has developed into acceptable reality, but the word stuck. So the "social myth" means *that* code of ideas by which the men and women of a society live and die. The ideal criterion for the validity of this code is that if a man should follow this myth and through it come to personal ruin or even death, he will die believing that it was his fault and not that of the code. Do we have a code on which we could lean like that? We used to, but we see it drying up before our eyes. What must such a code be like? The items that are mentioned here have been tested before by many professional groups and have been proven over time.

First: *Knowledge is power.* This old cliché has now surely been impressed on all of our minds. The infant, in becoming aware of his environment, sees his parents brutally engaged in acquiring, discussing, and using new powers. It is a characteristic of today's man that he must believe in what is going to be right, and he recognizes that all capability to help himself and the people around him to get in harmony with the cybernetic structure of his society comes out of the power of his knowledge and the skill to use it.

Second: *The joy is the becoming,* not in the being. Many of us know what a strong opiate is the ecstasy of new insight and the expanding vistas of knowledge and power which it brings. This must be taught to all of the people, and certainly must be taught to all of the professional class, because only through social approval, fortification, and orientation can a man happily and vigorously bear the burden of learning, which is the only way by which he can escape obsolescence. This is observable by looking at the poverty program for engineers, many of whom are kept in the echelon reserved for technicians.

The ecstasy of new insight and new powers through knowledge must become the central goal of experience for such a society. As you serve, so shall you be free in a dense society. Consequently, a free man is a man who serves so well that through spontaneous interaction those around him need only to know his wish to make it come true. This will be the real freedom. And some rudiments of this can be seen already in our society, although it is complicated by the imperfect transducer* called money.

In the old pioneer days, man interacted mainly with nature. Now the loops all come from man to man in inter-personality or inter-group interaction. Sometimes this idea is called the commutation of the souls in spite of the transcendental meaning of this colloquial term—a soul being, in this nomenclature, the individual conscious entity of which we are all aware. In the language base one does not define it this way. Soul "A" operating on soul "B" under certain boundary conditions is going to be exactly equivalent to soul "B" operating on soul "A." This is an essential condition to the dynamism of a society in which the person who may be an "ivory tower specialist" or almost isolated in one day could be the essential leader in the social effort the next day. Social mobility and the adaptability of a society are essentially connected, and this is consistent with our present behavioral make-up.

If anyone will follow this code of changeability conscientiously and to a greater extent than he has in the past, he will be richer and happier. In other words, the motivation gradient is downhill on a potential incline. You can get there from here because you will be rewarded and reinforced for the original effort.

How now does creativity enter into this picture? In a dynamic society of the future, the experience of encountering a novel situation which one has never learned to master before will be a common one. That is true of creativity, or what it means today. For example, if one walks up to the door and grasps the knob and turns the handle, the door opens; no problem. If the door knob comes off in your hand, creativity begins. For success in such a society where problem solving is the prime human attribute, one has to have a certain potential, some native ability, preparation, education and experience. But this is not the kind of experience that the infant has, because he is very creative when he discovers his arms and legs and the bars on his crib. As long as one is trained to maintain himself at the point where he can move on and around the perimeter of common human knowledge, he is not well prepared to stand on his own in a cybernetic society.

Your worth starts with the way you encounter a problem. Normally you try to solve it the way that you think it ought to be solved. But it does not work. This then is the error signal in the loop. Then adaptive behavior sets in. Today's man reacts to lack of accomplishment with frustration, which follows the initial failure. Then he might throw things, a syndrome called the "fight or flight." He may "sour grapes" it and then go away; he may try to go around the other end to get there, or there might be other avoidance reactions. You try and fail, and try and fail, and try and fail. This is what the psychologists have learned about the men who are creative in research. They are capable of keeping their orientation under prolonged, repeated frustration.

It has been a very popular idea promoted by some of our young scientists and also some young engineers that, "If you just give me a fine soft chair with a big plate glass window overlooking the beach somewhere, I will think great thoughts and the company will get a big profit." Well, that has been tried and it just isn't so, for in most of the cases the guy goes to sleep instead.

The fact of the matter is that the road to creativity runs right along the rim of hell, as it always has and probably always will. Necessity and stress are the powers of invention, as they have been in evolution.

Finally, let us look at insights. They can be genuine, convenient, or misguided. Humanity has often been victimized by them, especially when they occur in men who have great powers. Now, however, we have a weapon to defend us against abuse—The Scientific Method. You can verify the truth-value of most insights with an organized effort, and there is where organization and cooperative effort come to a great advantage.

Let us now shift from the problem of the individual to that of men working together in groups. All goal-seeking entities, whether units or groups, are servo systems. We inherited this hierarchical structure from the chickens and the dog packs; the apes have it too. But let us look at it from the standpoint of an engineer. Suppose you are not a servo-mechanical engineer, and a customer comes to the door and he says, "I need a mechanism that will permit me to steer my way down a crooked road through the fog where the road is lined with trees. Now I will give you the servo diagram that you are to use for this purpose. Furthermore, of course, this thing is going to go at an ever-increasing speed." You probably would refuse to engage in any such nonsense. But there is a way that we can do it. There it is, an open servo route and a multi-stage power amplifier, which is capable of repeated performance. And this can be applied to small group interactions.

Now, in the given situation, what does such a thing do? It is obvious. There is an open route, the thing has its servos connected; it has large time constants; it is lazy; and it is made of unreliable, mismatched components. Does this not remind you of group dynamics? The transfer function, without which it cannot operate at all, is called the Standard Operating Procedure. It has memories, logic, some informal stabilization which would not meet Nyquist's* approval, and loops, which in case of a company are usually called "staff." The adaptability of the device is limited by the Standard Operating Procedure. If there occurs an input signal in real hierarchy that doesn't match the Standard Operating Procedure, it trips the fail-safety and stops the action. In this case, when we are dealing with a large organization, there is no use putting a stress on a bureaucracy, because it is perfectly elastic in its homeostasis. It will just wait for you to get tired of applying stress—and then it will snap right back to where it was. A newer technique is required.

For better adaptation of an individual to the rapid change, there seems to be some help. Cybernetically speaking, it is advisable that about once a year, one should sum up the purposes: "What am I trying to make the world do and be?—and what am I trying to make myself do and be?" Then one should examine one's group belongings, and create new ones; maybe even create new small groups. This is very useful in helping to deal with the changing purposes in the kaleidoscopically changing situation which goes on. On the other hand, innovations can be very expensive. Many of our present organizations are trying and are also suffering from this, because one can progress himself broke in a hurry. Could it not be that the United States is progressing itself broke at this moment? Unless more people start thinking systems-analytically, and follow the cybernetic approach to govern our society, it might happen soon.

With logistics there is less trouble. It changes slowly enough, so that one can use hierarchies as safeguards. Its receipt, storage, repair, distribution and surveying of things is a repetitive job in a more or less steady state. There is some economic improvement possible by using linear programming.

So far we have regarded man mainly as an individual component in a system, but also as the whole model of the human opportunity and predicament in the subset called Western World.

We discussed briefly whether our country was progressing itself broke or not, especially with the encouragement and the insinuations of our enemies. They would like to see this happen. The time has come that our major attention should be centered around the *economics of information.* This new value type may be embodied in X-15's or computer hardware, or maybe in PERT programs,* scheduling, and the hectic, often wasteful testing that goes with the development process. *The end product of all of this is always information.* Presently this country spends about 17 billion dollars a year for the production of new information. What makes information worthwhile? What is its value under any circumstances? What are its economic uncertainties? Information has also some interesting properties as a merchandise, as an economic good. For instance, it has an infinite shelf life, without deterioration. Obsolescence does not mean deterioration in its truth-value. It is only a reduced probability for the need of its recall. Today we are proliferating information, and call it a virtue, regardless of the cost. Are we not over-producing information, as we are doing with population or some other merchandise? Do we really know what we are doing? Should we not better give information production a good hard look from the point of view of cybernetics and fit it into the system of our social dynamics?

GLOSSARY

"A"

ABSCISSA: in a graph, the horizontal axis or coordinate. (p. 174)

ACTION POTENTIAL: the small electrical current generated by the action of a muscle. (p. 47)

A/D CONVERTER : analog to digital converting equipment used in computer technology. (p. 167)

ALGORITHMS: a system of instruction which describes unambiguously and accurately an interaction which is equivalent to a given type of flux of intelligence and a subsequent, controlled activity. (p. 25)

AMOEBOID MOTION: movement of single cell protista, such as an amoeba. (p. 103)

ANTHROPOCENTRIC: having man as the center of a problem. (p. 29)

ANTHROPOMETRY: the science of human bodily measurements. (p. 19)

ANTIBIAS NETWORK: electronic network which automatically corrects a deviation from the predetermined function. (p. 83)

ANTI-MATTER: fundamental atomic nuclear particles with opposite electrical charge. (p. 43)

ASHBY, ROSS: contemporary British neurologist and famous cybernetician. (p. 59)

"B"

BAND-WIDTH: electromagnetic signals which have wavelengths which fall within given limits. (p. 57)

BAYES SOLUTION: mathematical instrument in probability; deals with *a posteriority* functions. (p. 91)

BERNARD, CLAUD: French physiologist of the 19th century. (p. 41)

BICEPS BRACHII: muscle in the upper arm, which bends the under arm. (p. 47)

BINARY DIGIT: numbers in the binary system. (p. 15)

BIOCATALYST: a substance which activates or stimulates a biochemical reaction. Hormones, vitamins and enzymes are all biocatalysts. (p. 153)

BIODYNAMICS: the science dealing with the physical activities of bodily mechanisms. (p. 19)

BIOLOGICAL SPREAD: due to the great variability of man, its functions are in clusters of data. (p. 21)

BIONIC DEVICE: artifacts, sometimes implantable into the body, which simulate organismic functions. (p. 93)

BIONICS: the science of simulating organismic functions by electronic or other types of devices. (p. 5)

BIT-VALUE: "bit" is the abbreviation of "binary digit" and is a certain probability which constitutes the unit of information. (p. 160)

"BLACK BOX": professional term for a device which contains unknown components. It accepts signals and transforms them. By varying the input and observing the output, one can conclude about the nature of the components.(p. 136)

BREMERMAN, HANS: contemporary mathematician. Recently at the Univ. of California in Los Angeles. (p. 58)

"C"

CAUSAL FIELD: the spatio-temporal matrix of an event. (p. 49)

CENTRAL LIMIT THEOREM: in probability theory; that the sum of a number of independent random variables, having a finite average, will approach a normal distribution as the number of variables approaches infinity. (p. 135)

CERENKOV RADIATION: visible radiation given up by photons losing their energy by attenuation. (p. 39)

CHANNEL PERMEABILITY: the capacity of a medium in carrying the maximum amount of information. (p. 69)

CHEMORECEPTION: combined smell and taste sensation. (p. 154)

CHOLINESTERASE: enzyme interacting with choline in the synaptic activity of nerves. (p. 154)

CLYDE MOOD SCALE: a self-administered check list with self-rating. Used for the self-evaluation of astronaut performance. (p. 172)

CONDITIO SINE QUA NON: the absolutely necessary condition. (p. 51)

CONTACT ANALOG: visual information display developed for the Navy. The computer generated symbols which resemble a real flight path which is used as flight guidance. (p. 69)

COPEPOD: one-eyed microscopic marine animal, part of the plankton. (p. 146)

"D"

D/A CONVERTER: digital to analog converting device used in computers. (p. 167)

db: decibel measure of loudness. Logarithmic function of sound pressure difference. (p. 83)

DECISION FUNCTION: mathematical expression for the description of a certain part of the process in decision-making. (p. 91)

DELAYED TIME: information transmission where a human is involved. (p. 74)

DERIVATIVE FEEDBACK TERMS: rates of changes in feedback. (p. 85)

DIODE: electronic component, vacuum tube. (p. 92)

DRIESCH, HANS: German philosopher and biologist. His famous book: *Philosophie des Organischen*, 1902. (p. 33)

"E"

EFFECTORS: generally referred to in physiology as nerve endings in sensory end-organs. (p. 60)

ELMER AND ELSIE: Cybernetic devices simulating certain animal functions. (p. 45)

ENDO-ENVIRONMENT: man's physical and chemical milieu inside his body. (p. 122)

ENERGY LIBIDO: the free energy available for a certain activity. (p. 152)

ENTROPY: in thermodynamics the energy lost from a system. In information theory the measure of the efficiency of transmission as code or language, indicating initial uncertainty, or "noise." (p. 40)

EPIGENETIC: caused mainly by genetic factors. (p. 136)

EPIPHENOMENON: caused by another phenomenon. (p. 112)

EXOBIOLOGY: extra-terrestrial life. (p. 49)

EXO-ENVIRONMENT: man's world outside his body, which includes the inside of his digestive tract. (p. 3)

EXOGEN NEED: a need which originates from outside of the system. (p. 86)

"F"

FEEDBACK: the return to the input of a part of the output of a machine, system or process. (p. 44)

FLIP-FLOP CIRCUITS: electronic device, half of which is conducting; the other half is not and the functions can be switched. (p. 40)

FORCING FUNCTION: mathematical expression which refers to an external variable which brings about a predetermined action in the system. (p. 129)

FOURIER ANALYSIS: method of reducing complex interactions into a set of functional dependencies. (p. 55)

FREE RADICALS: incomplete chemical compounds which exist for a long time only at the temperature of space. At higher temperatures they combine with other atoms immediately. (p. 47)

FUNCTION BANKS: predetermined and precomputed dependent variables which are stored in computer memory. (p. 21)

"G"

GADOMSKI: contemporary astronomer. (p. 50)

GAME THEORIES: mathematical instrument in probability used in models of competition. (p. 91)

GAMOV, GEORGE: Russian born physicist at Univ. of Colorado (deceased) famous for his popularized science books. (p. 43)

GATELL'S SIXTEEN PERSONALITY FACTOR INVENTORY: a part of the personality test battery, which assumes sixteen relatively independent personality factors and evaluates each subject on a relative scale. (p. 172)

GENERAL SYSTEMS: related to cybernetics; deals with complex, interacting components and organized wholes and applies them to concrete phenomena. (p. 6)

GENOTYPE: a shared genetic characteristic or the sharing group. (p. 121)

GESTALT THEORY: established in psychology in Germany in 1890, deals with groups of organized picture elements with system effects which are more than the sums of their parts. (p. 16)

"H"

HAECKELIAN MONISM: Haeckel's (1885) mechanistic philosophy of man, which negates spiritualism. (p. 29)

"HANDS-ON" PROGRAMMING: manual operation in the programming process in the "soft ware" of computers. (p. 167)

HEURISTIC: serving to stimulate investigation or discovery (also "educated guess"). (p. 9)

HOI POLLOI: the mass of the people. (p. 41)

HOMEOKINETIC: dynamic equilibrium in living organisms. (p. 178)

HOMEOSTASIS: self-organizing, self-maintaining equilibrium or organismic functions. Applicable also to mechanical, etc. systems. (p. 41)

HOMO COELORUM: space man; man of the heaven. (p. 54)

"I"

ID: the fundamental unit of personality from which derive the ego and libido. (p. 105)

IMPRINT STATE: stage of the young infant, when informations are mostly associated with the mother. (p. 100)

INERTIAL GUIDANCE PLATFORM: more or less stable directional reference with three mutually perpendicular giros as essential components. (p. 45)

INFORMATION FLUX: total flow of information per unit time. (p. 16)

INPUT-OUTPUT DEVICES: computer accessory equipment which accepts transmitted information for a computer, and displays retrieved and processed data. (p. 7)

INTELECTRONICS: the science of artificial intelligence achieved by special electronic circuitry, resembling a brain-like structure. (p. 6)

INTELLIGENCE AMPLIFIERS: electronic equipment or special computer which can aid man to arrive at valid decisions in a short time. (p. 134)

INVERTASE: enzyme in the stomach of the honey bee which splits disaccharides into monosaccharides. (p. 153)

IN VITRO: (Latin) in glass. (p. 33)

ITERATIVE INTEGRATING TECHNIQUE: solving certain integrals by using approximate functions and repeating the process for refining the solutions. (p. 167)

"J"

JEANS, SIR JAMES: English astronomer, contemporary. (p. 42)

JOUVET, M.: French physiologist and psychologist, interested in sleep. (p. 102)

"L"

L'ART POUR L'ART: (French) art for the sake of art. (p. 21)

LEONTIEFF: contemporary mathematician and statistician. (p. 124)

LICENTIA SCIENCIAE: (Latin) the liberty of the scientist. (p. 49)

LINEAR PROGRAMMING: mathematical approach developed for the optimization of technological and human sequential activities. (p. 15)

LOBOTOMY: mechanical destruction of certain lobes of the brain in case of severe psychosis. (p. 109)

LOGIC ELEMENTS: electronic components, used in computers. Termed "and," "or," "nor," referring to the logic of the signals to which they react. (p. 75)

LUMEN: the inner diameter of a tube. (p. 41)

"M"

MACHINA DOCILIS: learning machine. (p. 45)

MACHINA JUDICATRIX: decision-making machine. (p. 45)

MACHINA SPECULATRIX: thinking machine. (p. 45)

MACROCOSMOS: large world, or universe. (p. 38)

MARKOV-CHAIN: mathematical instrument in probability whereby the outcome of any trial depends on the outcome of the directly preceding trial. (p. 17)

MATERIALISTIC DIALECTICIAN: Marxist philosophers. (p. 130)

MATRIX: inert medium or structure which is the container or vehicle of a significant entity. In mathematics a grid of values which can be expressed also by differential equations. (p. 20)

MECHANO-RECEPTORS: sense organs in the skin which detect pressure changes. (p. 73)

MESON PHYSICS: physics of particles intermediate in mass between the electron and the proton. (p. 39)

METAZOIC ORGANISM: multi-cellular organisms, as an animal or plant. (p. 32)

MICRURGY: micro-surgery, operation under the microscope. (p. 49)

MILLILAMBERT: unit of surface brightness. One lambert equals one lumen per cm^2. (p. 94)

MINIMAX SOLUTION: mathematical instrument in probability, which minimizes the maximum risk. (p. 91)

MINSKY: contemporary roboticist at M.I.T. (p. 61)

MNEMOTECHNIQUE: a method which facilitates the memorizing of information. (p. 25)

MODALITIES: in psychology refers to the perception of the senses. (p. 69)

MONISM: materialistic philosophy of Haeckel referring to life as a complex machine. (p. 29)

MUTAGENIC: chemical and physical factors which, in influencing the genes, cause mutations. (p. 148)

"N"

NARROW BAND-PASS FILTERS: electronic device which prevents the flow of signals except those within restricted wave-length bands. (p. 20)

NATURE-MACHINE-MAN TRIADIC: a triple system involving simultaneously man, machine and nature. (p. 3)

NEGENTROPY: refers to the energy requirement of systems which move from disorganized to organized states. Also, the accumulating of information is connected with it. (p. 139)

NEUROGLIA CELLS: special nerve cells. (p. 103)

NEURO-HUMORAL SECRETION: hormones produced and secreted by nerve cells. (p. 105)

NEURONS: nerve cells. (p. 13)

NEUTRINO: a neutral atomic particle of mass less than any other nuclear constituents. (p. 54)

NOOSPHERE: Chardin's term for near-space to Terra. (p. 5)

NYQUIST: physicist who developed the requirements for the stability of automatic controls. (p. 184)

"O"

OPEN-LOOP SYSTEM: a dynamic system with feedback capability which, however, has a continuing influx and output of information. (p. 24)

OPERATOR: mathematical term for certain functions. (p. 152)

OUTPUT DEVICES: computer sub-system for displaying computational results. (p. 7)

"P"

PARASYMPATICUS: nervous system also called vagus, opposing the nervous activities of the sympaticus system. (p. 160)

PARI PASSU: (Latin) looking at the component in judging the whole. (p. 33)

PARS PRO TOTO: (Latin) using a part to refer to the whole. (p. 20)

PARTHENOGENESIS: generating living cells without parents. (p. 40)

PAVLOVIAN: Pavlov, Russian experimental psychologist. (p. 45)

PENTOMIC AND PENTANA CONCEPTS: special tactical battle field configurations with deep mutual penetration. (p. 66)

PERCEPTION RATE: the flux of bits of information which are assimilated by the mind. (p. 68)

PERT: Program Evaluation and Review Technique is an optimizing procedure for time and cost in complex sequential activities. (p. 185)

PHARYNGEAL GLAND: refers to the gland located in the vicinity of the pharynx of some insects. (p. 153)

PHENOTYPIC: hereditary characteristics which are observable. (p. 121)

PI-THEOREM: used in dimensional analysis to form non-dimensional parameters of physical phenomena, such as in fluid mechanics. (p. 174)

PLANKTON: one-celled animal or plant organisms in the sea. The lowest element of the food-chain. (p. 147)

POLYMORPHIC SWITCH: switch which can select or connect many functions. (p. 18)

PONS: means "bridge," refers to the posterior part of the brain. (p. 103)

PRAGMATOSCOPE: cybernetic device, developed by the author, which permits the utilization of larger amounts of information for decision-making than the human brain can normally manipulate. (p. 16)

PRINCIPLE OF UNCERTAINTY: limits of the precision of measurements (Heisenberg). (p. 54)

PRODIGALITY: extravagant spending. (p. 152)

"PROGRAMS": in missilry refers to the stage of the flight, when a predetermined automatic guidance system in the missile is in operation. (p. 79)

PROPRIOCEPTIVE: sensory stimulus, which originates within various tissues, e.g., tendon, muscle, etc. (p. 142)

PSYCHOKINETICS: moving things with mental power. (p. 43)

PSYCHOMOTOR FUNCTION: transferring mental function into mechanical movements of the body. (p. 18)

PULSE–HEIGHT ANALYZER: device which reacts to a signal of predetermined amplitude. (p. 5)

"Q"

QUANTUM RESTRICTIONS: stable states of atomic elements described in quantum mechanics. (p. 58)

QUASI-SINUSOIDAL: snake-motion-like wave form which is not a perfect sine-wave. (p. 174)

"R"

RASHEVSKY: founder of the subscience Mathematical Biophysics, Prof. of the Univ. of Chicago. (p. 152)

READ-OUT: type of system information output of computers. (p. 145)

REAL TIME: information transmitted by any parts of the electromagnetic spectrum without the intervention of man. Such as, light, radio signals, electric current, etc. (p. 74)

RECTIFIER: in electronics refers to a device which changes alternating current to direct current. (p. 40)

RENDEMENT: yield. (p. 48)

REQUISITE VARIETY: law defined by Ross Ashby for the theory of regulation. Deals with the need of a minimum number of parameters to satisfy the requirements of self-organizing systems. (p. 48)

RHOMBENCEPHALIC: part of the brain developed in the embryonic hind-brain. (p. 103)

RIBOSOME: site of the synthesis of complex pentoses (sugars) in the cell nucleus. (p. 145)

ROBOTICS: the science of intelligent, partially self-organizing automats. (p. 53)

RODS AND CONES: light sensing nerve endings in the retina. (p. 71)

"S"

SAGE SYSTEM: information processing system for air defense in which the flux of information is subdivided and processed by a number of humans and then reunited on an information display. (p. 69)

SATELLITE RESEARCH: space research performed through the observation of satellites. (p. 31)

SERVO MECHANISM: mechanical or electrical device which, as a slave-drive, follows exactly the motions of another device to which it is coupled. (p. 176)

SET-NOMENCLATURE: refers to the symbols of the set theory. (p. 163)

SHANNON'S THEOREMS: mathematical expressions of information. Introduces entropy in the probability of letters or words occurring in messages. Deals also with problems of coding and encoding. (p. 48)

SINE QUA NON: (Latin) condition without which something cannot exist. (p. 4)

SOCRATIAN TYPE OF INSTRUCTION: the type of instruction which Socrates used in teaching, mostly argumentative. (p. 24)

SYNAPTIC DISCONNECTS: the small gaps between the junctions of nerves. (p. 103)

SZONDI TEST: psychological test for behavioral background. Also, called "fate analysis." (p. 162)

"T"

TELENCEPHALIC: forebrain. (p. 103)

TELEOLOGY: the doctrine which states that in Nature purpose is often revealed by the form. (p. 29)

TELE-SUMMONER: tactile signaling device designed by the present author, worn as a watch and actuated by a single radio signal. (p. 86)

TEMPORAL-OPERATIONAL UNIVERSE: operation performed in a closed environment and in the time function. (p. 99)

TIME-COMPRESSED ENVIRONMENT: in which the normal time sequence is shortened. (p. 67)

TRANSDUCER: device which transforms one type of energy or physical mode into another. (p. 182)

TRANSFER FUNCTION: sequence of transforms of mental to physical bodily events, if applied to biology. It has also mathematical and physical meaning. (p. 4)

TUNNEL DISPLAY: visual information display in which a series of rings form a virtual tunnel as guidance for airplanes. (p. 69)

TURING MACHINE: mathematical description of universal automata which could do anything with information that any other machine can do. They can reproduce themselves and machines which are more complex than themselves. It can, in a simple form, be regarded as the forerunner of computers. (p. 77)

"V"

VIRTUAL MESONS: nuclear components with unusual characteristics. (p. 54)

VOICE CONTROL: device which reacts to the human voice and can be controlled by it. (p. 4)

VON BERTALANFFY: Ludwig von Bertalanffy, pioneer of the organismic view in biology and the symbol manipulating in man for interpretation of his experiences; von Bertalanffy is also the founder of General Systems Theory. (p. 66)

"W"

WALTER, GREY: contemporary English neurologist and cybernetician, designer of bionic devices. (p. 45)

WIENER, NORBERT: one of the founders of modern cybernetics (deceased) (p. 6)

"Z"

ZERO TURNOVER RATE: organ in which deteriorated or dead cells do not regenerate. (p. 39)

ZERO-SUM TWO-PERSON GAME: used in game theory, for games in which the gain of one player is the loss of the other player. (p. 91)

SELECTED REFERENCES
(In Suggested Order of Reading)
Chapter 1.
(Cybernetics)

Amosov, N.M. *Modeling of Thinking and the Mind*, 1967.

Rose, J. (editor) *Survey of Cybernetics*, 1969.

Rose, J. (editor) *Progress of Cybernetics* (Vols. 1, 2, 3), 1970.

Oldenburger, R. (editor) *Optimal and Self-Optimizing Control*, 1966.

Yakubaitis, E.A. *Fundamentals of Engineering Cybernetics*, 1965.

Masturzo, A. *Cybernetic Medicine*, 1965.

Pask, G. *An Approach to Cybernetics*, 1968.

Singh, J. *Great Ideas in Information Theory, Language and Cybernetics*, 1966.

Arbib, M.A. *Brains, Machines and Mathematics*, 1965.

Ivakahenko, *et al. Cybernetics and Forecasting Techniques*, 1967.

von Foerster, *et al. Principles of Self-Organization*, 1962.

von Bertalanffy, L. *Robots, Man and Minds*, 1967.

Porter, A. *Cybernetics Simplified*, 1969.

Maltz, M. *Psycho-Cybernetics*, 1960.

Wiener, N. *My Connection with Cybernetics*, 1958.

Ashby, W.R. *Requisite Variety and its Implication for the Control of Complex Systems*, 1956.

Wiener, N. *Cybernetics*, 1948.

von Foerster, *et al. Purposive Systems*, 1968.

Parin, V. *Introduction to Medical Cybernetics*, 1966.

Pierce, J.R. *Symbols, Signals and Noise*, 1961.

(Bionics)

Marteka, V. *Bionics*, 1965.

Milhorn, H.T. *Application of Control Theory to Physiological Systems*, 1966.

Engelbart, D.C. *Augmenting Human Intellect*, 1962.

Gilstrap, *et al. Compilation of Biological Laws, Effects and Phenomena with Associated Physical Analogs*, 1964.

Rosenblatt, F. *Perceptron Simulation Experiments*, 1960.

Gerardin, L. *Bionics*, 1968.

von Steinbuch, K. *Automat und Mensch*, 1965.

Gutchin, I.B. *Bionics and Reliability*, 1967.

Grubov, V.A. *Self-Organizing Control Systems*, 1967.

(Intelectronics)

Fogel, *et al. Artificial Intelligence through Simulated Evolution*, 1966.

Gunther, G. *Das Bewusstsein der Maschinen*, 1957.

Sluckin, W. *Minds and Machines*, 1960.

Watzlawick, P. *et al. Pragmatics of Human Communication*, 1967.

von Neumann, J. *Theory of Self-Reproducing Automata*, 1966.

Wooldridge, D.E. *Mechanical Man*, 1968.

Tart, C.T. *Altered States of Consciousness*, 1969.

Bell, D.A. *Intelligent Machines*, 1962.

Carne, E.B. *Artificial Intelligence Techniques*, 1965.

Fry, E.B. *Teaching Machines and Programmed Instruction*, 1963.

Chapter 2.

Joseph, R.D. *Contributions to Perceptron Theory*, 1960.

Buckley, W. *Modern Systems Research for the Behavioral Scientist*, 1968.

Chapter 3.

Shannon, C.E. *et al. Mathematical Theory of Communication*, 1949.

Adler, I. *Thinking Machines*, 1961.

Ashby, W.R. *Design for a Brain*, 1952.

Brillouin, L. *Mathematics, Physics and Information*, 1958.

Khinchin, A.I. *Mathematical Foundations of Information Theory*, 1957.

Abrahamson, N. *Information Theory and Coding*, 1963.

Kullback, S. *Information Theory and Statistics*, 1959.

Chapter 4.

Darne, F.R. *Advances in Techniques for Large Dynamic Display Devices*, 1965.

Hobbs, L.C. *Technologies for 1970 Era Practical Display Systems*, 1965.

Poole, H.H. *Fundamentals of Display Systems*, 1966.

Corbin, H.S. *A Survey CRT Display Consoles*, 1965.

Keast, D.N. *Survey of Graphic Input Devices*, 1967.

Overton, J.D. *et al. A Real-Time Display System for Ground Monitoring of Manned Space Flight*, 1967.

Jacobs, J.F. *Design Approach for Command and Control*, 1964.

Hoover, R.A. *The Houston Mission Control Center*, 1965.

Dertoyzos, M.K. *et al. A Parametric Graphical Display Technique for On-Line Use*, 1966.

Sutherland, I.E. *A Man-Machine Graphical Communication System*, 1963.

Engelbart, D.C. *et al. Study for the Development of Human Intellect Augmentation Techniques*, 1967.

Hall, D.J. *Programmer's Guide for the Man-Computer Display Facility*, 1967.

Baradar, J. *Visual Presentation of Flight Simulators*, 1965.

Nathan, R. *Digital Video-Data Handling*, 1966.

Chapter 5.

Adams, O.S. *et al. Prolonged Human Performance as a Function of the Work-Rest Cycle*, 1961.

Adler, E. *The Localization of a Sleep Syndrome*, 1924.

Aleksandrova, L.I. *The Role of Normal Sleep in the Preservation of Neuroses*, 1955.

Arnold, M.B. *On the Mechanism of Suggestion and Hypnosis*, 1959.

Atkinson, J.B. *Anatomy and Physiology of the Sleep Mechanism*, 1947.

Kleitmann, N. *Sleep and Wakefulness,* 1963.

Bartley, S.H. *et al. Fatigue and Impairment in Man*, 1947.

Boas, E.P. *The Heart Rate During Sleep*, 1929.

Davis, P.A. *Effects of Acoustic Stimuli on the Waking Human Brain,* 1939.

Jouvet, M. *Telencephalic and Rhombencephalic Sleep in the Cat*, 1961.

Kamiya, J. *Behavioral, Subjective and Physiological Aspects of Drowsiness and Sleep*, 1961.

King, C.D. *Dream and the Problem of Consciousness*, 1946.

Mott, F. *Sleep, Sleeplessness and Sleepiness*, 1924.

Schmidt, H. *The Reticular Formation and Behavioral Wakefulness*, 1957.

Zubeck, J.P. *et al. Intellectual Changes During Prolonged Perceptual Isolation*, 1960.

Chapter 6.

Merton, R. *Social Theory and Social Structure*, 1949.

Piaget, J. *Logic and Psychology*, 1957.

Young, K. *Social Psychology*, 1930.

White, W. *The Psychology of Dealing with People*, 1941.

von Foerster, H. *et al. Purposive Systems*, 1969.

Linton, R. *The Cultural Background of Personality*, 1945.

Maier, N.R.F. *Frustration, the Study of Behavior Without a Goal*, 1949.

Hovland, C.I. *et al. Experiments on Mass Communication*, 1949.

Adorno, T.W. *et al. The Authoritarian Personality*, 1950.

Chapter 7.

Osborn, F. *Preface to Eugenics*, 1940.

Chapter 8.

Merton, R.K. *Social Theory and Social Structure*, 1949.

Coleman, J.S. *Introduction to Mathematical Sociology*, 1964.

Lawrence, D.H. *et al. Deterrents and Reinforcement*, 1962.

Homans, J.C. *The Human Group*, 1950.

Foskett, J.M. *Social Structure and Social Participation*, 1955.

Gross, N. *et al. On Group Cohesiveness*, 1952.

Stewart, J.Q. *A Measure of the Influence of the Population at the Distance*, 1942.

Chapter 9.

Vigdorovich, M.L. *Dialectic Materialism and Present-Day Natural Science*, 1965.

von Bertalanffy, L. *General Systems Theory*, 1968.

Deutsch, K. *The Nerves of Government*, 1963.

Wiener, N. *God and Golem, Inc.*, 1964.

Dahl, R. *Modern Political Analysis*, 1963.

Dechert, C.R. *The Social Impact of Cybernetics*, 1966.

Chapter 10.

Masturzo, A. (editor) *Cybernetic Basis of Modern Medicine*, 1964.

Aladjalova, N.A. *et al. Wondering Burst of Electric Potentials in Structures of the Brain*, 1964.

Aladjalova, N.A. *et al. Some Mechanism of the Slow Control Processes in the Brain*, 1962.

Grodins, F.S. *Control Theory and Biological Systems*, 1963.

du Buy, H.G. *Mitochondria of the Cerebral Cortex as Possible Sites of Mnemonic Functions*, 1964.

Dessau, E. *Medical Information Processing and the Use of Electronic Computers*, 1964.

Gawronski, P. *et al. The Modeling and Interpretation of Peripheral Muscle Control Systems*, 1964.

Goldacre, R.J. *Cybernetics of Cancer and Normal Growth*, 1964.

Huant, E. *Cybernetics of the Time-Sense*, 1964.

Korein, J. *et al. Computer Processing of Medical Data*, 1963.

Korein, J. *Towards a General Theory of Living Systems*, 1964.

Livanov, M.N. *Biological Aspects of Cybernetics*, 1962.

Masturzo, A. *Neurocybernetic Aspects of the Fundamentals of Reumatology*, 1963.

Nigro, A. *From the Reflex Arch to the Cybernetic Circuit*, 1964.

Chapter 11.

von Foerster, H. *et al. Principles of Self-Organization*, 1962.

Chapter 12.

Patton, R.L. *Insect Physiology*, 1963.

Wiglesworth, V.B. *The Control of Growth and Form*, 1959.

Counce, S.J. *Insect Embryogenesis*, 1961.

Chapter 13.

Brunswik, E. *Perception and Representative Design of Experiments*, 1956.

Helvey, T.C. *The Szondi Test*, 1967.

Chapter 14.

no references

Chapter 15.

Rosenberg, M. *Cognitive Structure and Attitudinal Affect*, 1956.

Cartwright, D. *Group Dynamics*, 1953.

Halpin, A. *The Leadership Behavior of School Superintendents*, 1956.

Baldwin, A. *et al. Patterns of Parent Behavior*, 1945.

Postman, L. *et al. Psychology in the Making*, 1963.

Barnard, C. *Functions of the Executive*, 1938.

Dahl, R.A. *The Concept of Power*, 1957.

Fiedler, F.E. *A Note on Leadership Theory*, 1957.

Osborn, A.F. *Applied Imagination*, 1957.

Godfrey, E. *et al. Boards, Management and Company Success*, 1959.

Chapter 16.

Novik, I. *Philosophical and Sociological Problems*, 1964.

Berg, A.I. *et al. Cybernetics, Thought and Life*, 1965.

Miller, R.W. *Schedule, Cost and Profit Control with PERT*, 1963.

Makower, M.S. *et al. Operational Research*, 1967.